A Memoir of Deafness

BAINY B. CYRUS

ISBN: 1450540317
ISBN-13: 9781450540315
Library of Congress Control Number: 2010900843

Bainy Cyrus' All Eyes was originally published in 2005 by Gallaudet University Press in an anthology titled Deaf Women's Lives: Three Self-Portraits.

To Diane Karas Cummings and Cheryl Robbins Johnston
for their everlasting friendships
To the Karas and Robbins families for their hospitality
during my Clarke years away from home
To Mom and Dad for their tremendous support and
unconditional love all these years
To my brothers Nash, Lindsay, and Harvey for their
uncanny ways of teaching me humor
Finally to my husband Steve for his survival with burnt dinners
while I was writing this book. . .

ACKNOWLEDGEMENTS

This memoir was first published in an anthology titled *Deaf Women's Lives: Three Self-Portraits* so I would like to thank Gallaudet University Press for its first printing. Ivey Pittle Wallace, Brenda Brueggemann, Lauren Kelley, Paula Campos, and the copyeditor by the name of Mary all did an excellent job of preparing my memoir *All Eyes* for the 2005 edition. The editing was done so well by Gallaudet University Press that I kept almost 100% of *All Eyes* original for this second printing, except for a few updates and additional characters. And again I want to thank Gallaudet for allowing me to republish *All Eyes* as a stand-alone edition.

There are also many other people I would like to thank for their support during my ten struggling years to get the original memoir published. Anne Kramer, who passed away in 2006, first taught me creative writing during our private sessions back in 1994 when I first wrote a novel based on deafness (Never published but actually a perfect warm-up for *All Eyes!*) Then I went on to take creative writing classes at Old Dominion University and cannot thank these professors enough for their encouragement (and yes, some criticism which is the best teacher for all writers!)

When researching my past at Clarke School, I flew up to Northampton in 1993 and stayed in one of the dorms on the campus for two days. The hospitality at Clarke was much appreciated and I was given a chance to observe ongoing education in my old classrooms. Of course, that brought back so many memories such as headphone pranks and old-fashioned oral training. Many of my old teachers including Marjorie Magner, Priscilla Pike, Bob Storm, Eleanor Jones, David Manning, Muriel Crockett, and Bill Blevins were all there, even after 40 plus years, to share great, often humorous, memories with me. Without them this book would not be possible.

Finally, I would like to thank my parents, brothers, Cheryl, Diane, and their families for sharing their stories, many of which I would never be able to remember. It took them a vast amount of time to read my first revision (a much longer version) and helped with corrections. They all made this memoir much more realistic and personal.

Finally, finally, I thank my husband Steve for his undying patience and support all these years. And he was the one that encouraged me to reprint *All Eyes* as a stand-alone edition and did all the dealings with Gallaudet University Press. I promise no more burnt dinners.

It was indeed a wondrous day for my mother, having finally gotten her wish after bearing a string of three wild little boys. Mom collapsed on the delivery table with a sigh of relief when she saw the absence of a tiny weenie as soon as I slipped out of her womb. As an adult, I can imagine that excitement with a chuckle, but I also wonder what it was like for my mother to be deceived with my normal appearance. Although no one knew at that time, I had been born with a hidden disability.

By the time I was eighteen months old, my parents sensed something wasn't right with me. My grandmother Donnie had long suspected that I didn't seem to act like any other baby so she urged Mom to take me to the family pediatrician. I did not demand as much attention as my brothers did. Nor was I aware of comings and goings in the house. I did not wail at the sound of the front door shutting, even with my playpen only ten feet away, and I never turned at my mother's homecoming. Most of all, I had not spoken a single word, not even "Ma" or "Dada," as I should have long ago. My brothers had not shown these "symptoms" when they were my age.

When Mom took me to the pediatrician, she was assured that I was still too young to talk and that I might have "the last child syndrome." That is, the baby in a particularly large family was usually spoiled as a result of constantly being waited on by older siblings who interpreted the baby's words. Nevertheless, Mom became increasingly concerned with my lack of speech. She brought me to the doctor for a couple more visits, only to be assured that I would eventually produce my first word out of the blue.

But Donnie wasn't convinced. "I don't believe it. There *is* something wrong with Bainy," she insisted to Mom and Dad. Hearing these words, Dad, who was a doctor specializing in internal medicine, began to think that his mother-in-law was right. Since he was out working all day, he hadn't seen enough of me to notice my lack of baby words. Yet, I always beamed at my dad's tickle game every evening as he rolled his finger around before zapping me in the tummy, eliciting giggling squeals from me.

Mom fearfully suspected mental retardation, but Dad didn't think so because he had seen me put toys together, most of the time, flawlessly. In fact, I was more coordinated with toys than my brothers. Donnie assumed that I was deaf because I had never turned in reaction to the door slamming. So she and Mom once again took me to the pediatrician and asked for hearing tests. Without hesitation he brought out a bell and rang it behind my back. *Ding, ding, ding.* Nothing. I hardly moved a muscle as I sat there and stared at my mother. Frowning, the pediatrician realized for the first time that there was definitely a problem. He decided to try making a louder sound. Standing behind me, he held an inflated balloon and burst it with a needle. *POP!* Still no response. My face remained blank, staring straight ahead. The pediatrician stepped back in concern. This time he knew better than to tell my mom to wait for my first word.

Finally, the pediatrician placed a tape recorder behind me and turned it on. It emitted the deep, rounded tones of a male voice. He increased its volume and inched it closer to me. I did look up with a puzzled frown, my eyes still transfixed on the wall ahead of me. After staring at me, the pediatrician hesitantly asked my mother, "Does she hug you?" Mom and Donnie were taken back by his question and wondered what a hug had to do with these hearing tests. Mom replied, "Of course, she hugs me. Just like any other child. Why did you ask?"

"She seemed to hear the tape recorder but didn't know where the sound came from. She could've turned her head to the recorder," the pediatrician said, obviously reluctant to add more details. What he had in mind was autism and he didn't want to upset Mom with his assumption. So he suggested that she take me to an otologist for more accurate hearing tests. My parents saved copies of medical reports written by the pediatrician and other doctors about my diagnosis. In those flimsy yellowed letters, the pediatrician described my actions to doctors at Johns Hopkins University Hospital. His typewritten words, fading over forty-five years, show that he really did care. Mom told me that this pediatrician expressed remorse for not noticing my abnormality sooner. I understand that back then in the early 1960s, pediatricians knew little about the symptoms of any disability.

More hearing tests were performed, eliciting very little response from me. The otologist believed I had a very definite loss, but he was uncertain about deafness because other conditions such as autism or aphasia could be possible. He explained that, like deafness, these other disabilities could show symptoms in toddlers such as not recognizing sounds and not developing speech. And it was too early to find out exactly what the problem was, he told my parents.

The otologist immediately referred me to the Speech and Hearing Center at Old Dominion University. There, an audiologist placed me in a small alcove, putting a headphone on my head, and began performing tests with an audiometer. He found that I responded to bell and flute sounds over 70 decibels between 500 and 2000 cycles per second. My response indicated that, at a high volume, I could hear low-frequency sounds better than high-frequency ones. That technical language may sound confusing to you, so I'll explain a little of it to you now and more later when I explain the oral education method. What is important to understand here is that a decibel is a measurement of loudness. The range runs from 0 decibels to 140 decibels. The level of 0 decibels represents the softest sound a typical ear can hear, like the sound of a pin dropping. And *that* is a normally hearing person's threshold. At the level of 55 decibels is loud conversational speech. The level of 75 decibels includes the sound of city traffic. The level of 140 decibels includes the sound of a jet engine at take-off. Well, the audiologist found that I could start hearing at 70 decibels in the low-frequency range.

However, the audiologist advised that no definite conclusions about hearing or not hearing could be made with certainty at the moment because of my young age. Instead, he suggested further observation of my responses before confirming the diagnosis. He then counseled Mom and Dad about speech stimulation, instructing them to talk to me as much as they could, only face to face. Knowing that this method of stimulating speech would be a burden at home, the audiologist suggested that I work with a speech therapist at Old Dominion. Mom and Dad agreed, eager for me to say *something*.

Several months passed, and all attempts at motivating me to vocalize and imitate vowels had been fruitless. Mary Jane, a speech therapist, had worked with me two or three days a week. I do vaguely remember her as an affectionate person who seemed to work awfully hard at motivating me. Mary Jane and I met again thirty years later at a coffee café and had a captivating conversation because she told me how everyone had believed that I had a complex communicative disorder. Deafness was the last thing on their list because I did have some hearing, particularly of loud sounds. Aphasia was what everyone assumed. This disorder, which is a complete absence of the communication and comprehension skills, provides an explanation for the child's failure to speak. An aphasic child cannot follow the meaning of the words he or she hears. According to Mary Jane, I showed these symptoms. She would set small things on the table and ask me to pick up a pen.

After many unsuccessful attempts, I would finally pick up the right item. But the next day, I'd completely forget. Not knowing what the "pen" looked like. Back to the drawing board. Mary Jane would have to start all over again. But she persevered.

As our therapy sessions progressed, Mary Jane realized that I watched her lips intently. I had finally lipread some words such as "yes" and "no." But still I couldn't vocalize. Instead, I began talking to myself silently in front of the mirror. The medical reports explain that I jabbered without any sound coming out of my mouth, making livid facial expressions and gestures. Boy, I must have looked nutty! But I had a perfect reason for my puppet-like actions. Because I didn't know that voices and moving lips were often associated together, I began to think it was natural for everyone to mouth words. No wonder I began to imitate facial expressions, especially Mom's. I'd just frown hard and shake my index finger up and down, babbling in silence. That's how Mom scolded me whenever I knocked over a glass of fruit drink or threw a plastic toy block. When scolded, I'd place my hands over my eyes. You guessed it, I didn't want to see my mother's lips!

Now I was two and a half years old and still not speaking. It was time to take me to Johns Hopkins Hospital which had pioneers in the field of deafness. That trip involved a four-hour drive to Baltimore, which would be the first of many in several months. To rule out autism, the local doctors made an appointment for us to meet with the specialist, also in Baltimore, who was famous for his research on autism. Mom and Dad feared a visit to the specialist because autism still might be a possibility. They knew autistic children lacked the ability to communicate and responded to sounds inappropriately. I had those symptoms; that's why Mom and Dad were scared out of their wits when they pulled up in front of a small colonial ranch house which was the specialist's office.

When we entered the foyer, the specialist descended the stairs with a broad grin and took one look at me in my dad's arms. He told Mom and Dad flat-out, "Bainy is not autistic." My parents were caught off guard and looked at each other. The specialist explained that he was watching by the window upstairs when we parked in front. When Dad removed me from the back seat, he knew instantly that I was not autistic. It was because I wrapped my arms around Dad's neck. If I were autistic, my arms would have gone limp or pushed Dad away. Much to my parents' relief, the specialist ruled out autism and, instead, suspected deafness after reading the reports from my local doctors. He didn't think I had aphasia because I watched lips.

That consultation led to the beginning of my numerous hearing tests spanning eight months at Johns Hopkins. The doctors found that, if I was visually engrossed, I didn't react to sound. However, if visual stimuli were removed and my attention was centered on listening, they could observe a variety of reactions to sound. Loud sounds of 70 decibels were enough to break into my visual preoccupation. I also reacted better to low-frequency sounds and required more decibels to hear high-frequency sounds.

Any of those doctors could have immediately suggested the use of amplification once the hearing impairment was diagnosed, but back in the 1960s, technology wasn't well advanced. Today, a deaf baby can even be diagnosed *on the day he or she is born*, thanks to high technology and a better understanding of deafness. Back then, the doctors didn't know the exact degree of my hearing loss, so they decided to use structured auditory listening games as a way to see whether I could discriminate sounds. They instructed Mom and Dad on how to stimulate my language and speech development at home by using a face-to-face only approach. We were sent home, knowing we would come back in the following weeks for more hearing tests.

Mom and Dad decided to rely on oralism because I had spent a considerable amount of time watching lips. That choice was fairly common for a hearing family who wanted their deaf child to be like them, able to speak. If I had come from a deaf family, it might have been different; sign language would have then been the likely choice. During our visit at the coffee café, Mary Jane went on to tell me that I still forgot to pick up a pen during one session after another. She explained that it was easy for me to forget new words when there was no auditory sense. Hearing babies, even those in wombs, remember the sounds of the words they hear, so they learn spontaneously. Deaf babies? No way. That's why a deaf child needs to be taught the same word over and over again, usually *thirty-five times.* In contrast, it takes only three repetitions for a hearing child to learn a word because it's much easier to remember the *sound* of each word. Hearing people learn by *hearing;* deaf people learn by *seeing.*

That's why I had to watch Mary Jane's and my mother's lips to understand speech. Actually, no one told me to lipread; I just happened to pick up the habit myself. Lips seemed to be the only thing moving on everyone's face, so why not watch the action? I just thought, and still think, lips are so full of character that they have a mind of their own. If lips are moving in a restricted way with frequent tightening, then whoa, I better step back and not aggravate that person. If lips are chapped, shredding like a river birch bark, then I assume that person must have spent a lifetime worshiping the sun.

Mom and Dad ordered the John Tracy correspondence course, which was designed for parents of oral-bound deaf children. This course was developed in the 1940s by the wife of Spencer Tracy, the movie actor who had a deaf son. The course encouraged my parents to teach me to associate things with lip movements. One of the step-by-step activities it recommended taught them to play matching games with me. Mom and Dad would scramble pairs of items on the floor, then pick up, for example, one shoe and mouth this word to me, and ask me to pick up another shoe in the midst of other items. I'd watch the lips carefully and pick up the right item.

However, I didn't always get things right. I would forget by the next day, and the same teaching would have to be started all over again. I bet my parents and Mary Jane wanted to wring my neck, but they knew that teaching a deaf child required top-level patience. The process was complex because so many words looked the same on the lips. To me, the spoken word "doll" may have looked like "dog" or "all." In the future, I would have to learn to watch the tongue formation in the mouth, the placement of teeth, and the vibrations of the cheeks.

Even the most skilled lipreaders get only between 30 percent and 40 percent of what is said, especially on fast-talking lips. That's why deaf people need to be spoken to slowly and clearly. Even though many words look alike on the lips, the lipreaders manage to understand by figuring out the right words to fit in, as I have learned over the years. For instance, you say, "Oh great!" On the lips, it could've been "grade" or "grain." Of course, I cannot hear the difference between those three words, but I can quickly grasp what the right word is given the context.

After taking more hearing tests at Johns Hopkins, I was given a final diagnosis: bilateral sensorineural hearing impairment. That diagnosis was what the doctors considered a very severe, close to profound, nerve deafness. The doctors suggested that I try mild amplification so I could learn to hear at a comfortable level and then eventually settle with a permanent hearing aid. The final diagnosis, of course, saddened my parents but what hit my mom twofold was the realization that I would never have a normal education and that her pregnancy was the cause of my deafness. She told me the first insight affected her most because she couldn't bear to send me away to a residential school. She and Dad were informed that I required long-term special education. Norfolk, Virginia, had no oral school that was appropriate. Mom was disheartened to learn that the closest reputable oral school, Clarke School, was 700 miles away in Massachusetts.

Mom was not too concerned about why I was born deaf because she had no plan to have any more children. Four was enough. She was too busy making sure my brothers and I stayed off the railroad tracks or didn't run through thorny bushes. Our health and safety occupied her mind. Still, the doctors were curious about my birth defect, and they had questions for my parents. Mom and Dad sat down, prepared to answer yes or no.

"Any history of genetic deafness in the family?" "No."

"Now about your child ...Any type of illness?" "No, just flu and colds, that's all."

"Has she had meningitis?" "No." "Scarlet fever?" "No."

"Middle ear infection?" "No." "Any ear injury?" "No."

"Did she develop skin rash?" "No." "Mumps?" "No."

"Okay...now about your pregnancy. Any trouble with it?" "No, it was uneventful."

"Mrs. Bilisoly, did you develop skin rash during your pregnancy?" "No."

"Did you have high fever during that time?" "Uh, yes. I was really ill for three or four days. The fever was very high. I remember it happened during the third month."

There it was. The real reason for my deafness. The doctors nodded at each other, one saying, "High fever during the third month could be the result of a case of rubella." Mom didn't know what to feel as she sat there confused and heartbroken. Dad, as a doctor, had heard of rubella but had not seen the symptoms among his patients before. He quickly assured Mom that it wasn't her fault, that rubella was something unavoidable like a flu bug, and that rubella was a form of viral infection known as German measles. This virus could have temporarily deprived my auditory nerves of oxygen, and the damage was done. It was the absolute cause of my hearing impairment, the doctors said. Mom knew she couldn't have done anything about this virus. I would never want her to feel guilty anyway.

Mom said my three brothers, the last one five years older than me, reacted well to my diagnosis because they were immediately informed that deafness was manageable. Nash, Lindsay, and Harvey, all before their adolescent phases, vowed that they would protect me but still treat me the same. They sure did. They made sure that I didn't get ridiculed or didn't date a jerk. But they still beat me up or turned my doll inside out, trying to turn me into a whiny little sister. Actually, I liked that because they were treating me like a normal person.

Lindsay told me that he noticed I was different before the diagnosis because I hardly ever cried. Possibly entranced by *The Twilight Zone* episodes, he even suspected I had supernatural powers, so he challenged his pal Hamil to hit me in the arm, bragging that I'd never cry. Hamil, though known as a prankster of the neighborhood, refused. Lindsay said to watch and socked me in the arm. He thought *Uh-oh* when my face slowly shriveled up, mouth arching downward, and I finally wailed WAAAAAAAAH! He felt bad enough about it that he grew up to be the most tenderhearted brother of all.

Things began to make more sense now that I was wearing a hearing aid. With this aid, I could turn up the volume to any level and feel comfortable with it. It was a shiny, silver Zenith Royal, the size of a dental floss pack, tucked in a white cloth pocket with straps all around my torso. I remember so vividly receiving this first hearing aid at age four and a half that I can play it back in my mind like a videotape. Lindsay came rushing into the house with excitement and dragged me outside in front of Dad who was surrounded by the entire family and some neighbors. After removing a new hearing aid from the bag, Dad placed the straps over me and then jiggled the earmolds into my tiny ears with my mother's help. He then glanced at me as if to say, "Are you ready?" and that caused everyone to circle around me like they were peering into a fish tank.

Dad turned on the hearing aid and said, "Hello, hello, hello." Bam! I heard his voice and grinned, driving everyone to excited laughter. Actually, that wasn't the first time I had heard a voice, since I had heard Mary Jane and others talking through mild amplification at Old Dominion. But this time was different— right here on the sidewalk—so many voices at the same time! Something else struck me, too. As I looked around with the hearing aid and straps and all, I realized that no one else had one on. I was the only one. At that moment, I learned of my deafness. Really, I had long thought everyone was just like me, not hearing anything. I even thought every single soul on earth took hearing tests as if they were a daily routine.

In the future, there would be questions and comments about the strange-looking thing on my chest. "What's that on you?" "What music are you listening to? Oh? It's not a radio?" "My gosh, it looks like a one-cup bra." Many more would follow. Years later, my sister-in-law Vickie found a picture of me wearing these straps and hesitantly asked why I had a harness. Her innocent question made me feel like a flesh-eating jungle beast caught in a net. I had never thought of that in the past!

Mom and Dad had made a decision to send me to Clarke School in Northampton, Massachusetts. Although they knew it was going to be painful not to have me home, they felt confident about this school that had earned an article in *National Geographic* for its reputable oral program. I had gone to Clarke for orientation and had been pleasant the whole time. But the second time, they *sent* me there, and I was a mess, screaming the whole way up. Mom was so frustrated because she couldn't tell me anything, even with my hearing aid, that would reassure me that I wasn't being left there for good. That's what made the situation so hard. Mom knew that I would be greatly upset being away from home, or worse yet, that I would be angry with her for "deserting" me. Being left at an unfamiliar place could be traumatic for any five-year-old. So the lack of communication wasn't the only factor.

My preschool photograph.

Whenever Mom tells the story about sending me to Clarke School, she dwells on the light blue smocked dress I had on. She had stitched it and was proud enough to parade me around in that dress nearly every day. Mom still has a portrait of me wearing the dress, sitting and smiling, taken before the screaming incident. I am sure she is reminded of my piteous screams every time she sees that portrait. She has said that seeing the dress became so disturbing after the incident that she never put it on me again.

When it was time for my parents to leave, I started to scream again. Miss Miller, my new teacher, restrained me from running after them. I don't remember any of that. But, whenever I think of the story Mom has told me many times, I can feel the powerful trauma of being separated from the two most important people in my life, particularly at such a young age of five.

ALL EYES

Clarke School was, and still is, a beautiful place with century-old brick buildings and gigantic pines. Hubbard Hall beckons with its green and white colonial sign that reads *Clarke School for the Deaf, established in 1867.* It was where I had my first class, all of us sitting on tiny wooden chairs arranged in a semicircular pattern facing Miss Miller so we could see her lips and one another's. Some of us fidgeted and others just stared ahead. One might think, oh, that looks like a normal preschool class. No, ours didn't look like one at all. Weighed down by ugly headphones, we all resembled miniature airline pilots. We each had our own volume boxes on the half-hexagonal stand behind us, and the main cord ran a good twenty feet from there to Miss Miller's mike around her neck. But still, the ample length would not prevent the many cord incidents ahead! Cords ran everywhere like a spider web, ready to trip or snare anybody.

That auditory training program was an extremely important step in the teaching of oralism. We would be learning not only to listen to the teacher's voice but also to hear our own voices. This method provided better amplification than a hearing aid because it cut off feedback. With this system, we would be better able to hear the vowels and consonants that we could not hear otherwise. Later on, we would learn how to make these sounds.

Crucial for our development was learning how to hear and recognize sounds with hearing aids. As preschoolers, we still had more to learn to use our residual hearing—what hearing we still had—to full advantage through our hearing aids. We would have to learn where the sounds came from, how they were made, what they meant. All of us had nerve deafness and, therefore, were unable to discriminate sounds, especially speech sounds, even with our hearing aids (which only made sound louder). In fact, we needed to *learn* to hear.

The hearing aid has its limitations. It cannot help the person hear everything. In most cases, the aid only reduces the hearing loss by 30–35 decibels. It's not at all like a pair of glasses that can correct vision. The aid also cannot help one discriminate sounds as well as hearing people can. It cannot cure distortion from a sensorineural loss that causes the voice to sound distorted and muffled. Even if a voice is very loud, its sound becomes worse and more distorted. These garbled sounds occur because many consonants are high-pitched and use frequencies for which I have the least hearing, as do most other deaf people.

I'll explain how I hear this sentence: *I like to play tennis but not with Betty who always beats me.* Well, all I can hear is *I lie oo ay enny buh nauh weh Beh-ee oo ahway bea me.* That's how most deaf people hear—and how they also *talk*, missing the high-pitched consonants. Imagine suddenly becoming deaf and then having to learn a foreign language. That's the same thing as being born deaf.

My classmates and I were about to begin a long, grueling process of oral education. Our hair would be slightly, if not permanently, squashed on the sides from wearing headphones every day. Auditory training was not a problem for me because I understood its necessity. I had grown to respect Clarke as a special school where I could always feel secure with kids like me, all of us wearing bulky hearing aids on our chests.

I remember wearing a headphone and sitting next to Miss Miller in front of a two-way mirror about three times a week. To begin teaching, Miss Miller gently took my hand and placed it on her cheek. Holding the mike under her chin, she began, "Ooooo … ooooo." With my hand on her cheek, I felt the vibration of speech through my hand. I could also hear Miss Miller's voice through my headphone. As a rule of oral education, I always had my eyes directed to the mirror. Miss Miller wouldn't let me gaze away to an inviting pile of toys in the corner or a housefly buzzing over us. Direct eye attention was what we needed so we could "hear" by lipreading.

Next came the spoken word "ball" along with a red item in Miss Miller's hand. With my hand on her cheek, I watched her lips form, "Buh, buh, *buh*," and then I tried to imitate her sound, uttering, "Bbbbuh" with the mike under my chin so I would learn to hear my own voice. Miss Miller, as many times as she had to, reminded me to look in the mirror to watch my own lips. She would hold up the ball and say, "Can you say 'ball'?" Once again, she would press my hand against her cheek and repeat this word. After many attempts, I would finally say, "Baaaaw," watching my lips in the mirror. Though the word was not spoken perfectly, Miss Miller praised me to boost my motivation. From her thirty-plus years of teaching oralism, she knew it was impossible for me to say "ball" with fullness the first time. It would take time and effort to learn a consonant such as *L*, which was almost invisible on the lips; I would eventually learn that a flap of the tongue over the upper teeth or slightly behind indicated this consonant. That's what lipreading is for—learning to "read" consonants.

Leonard House was a former family home on the edge of campus, a few minutes' walk to Hubbard Hall. This coed dormitory was only a hundred feet from the school infirmary that I always considered a haven. Whenever I sniffed or coughed, Miss Miller would sweep me off to the infirmary in concern, taking only a few long strides. I didn't mind going into this place drenched with the smell of ammoniac and full of red-eyed kids waiting either to be poked, rubbed, squeezed, hammered, and given baby aspirin or to be motioned down the hall to stay in a recovery room. Years later, I even considered faking illness so I could be placed in a comfortable hospital bed and read *Curious George*, away from the

classroom, acting sicker than having just a slight bad cold, honking and snorting loudly only when nurses walked in.

The girls' bedroom, across the hall from boys', was big enough
for eight of us, looking somewhat like an army barracks with
tiny cots. This room suited me fine, although I longed for my
own double bed at home. But still, I enjoyed the company of my
girlfriends. At night, Miss Miller, also residing at this dorm with
another teacher and a few housemothers, would tuck us in, saying
"good night." If one of us had trouble sleeping, she would place
our hand over her throat and sing a bedtime tune, knowing we
would feel the vibration of her voice. We never went to bed with
our hearing aids on since it would be uncomfortable to have our
earmolds pushed further in on the pillow.

My new friends and I hadn't yet learned to say names, only as-
sociating one another's faces, and other people's, with memorable
characteristics—the one with a zillion freckles, the one with buck
teeth, the one with Shirley Temple hair, the one with lopsided
glasses. Then we began to recognize names in writing, long before
we learned to say them. With fifteen of us in Leonard House,
we had to have every single one of our belongings labeled—even
our underwear—on which was either a sewn cloth name label or
inked letters of the last name. Leonard House was so laden with
written names that a visitor might suspect it was an FBI investiga-
tion lab.

Outside was the playground with the swing set, which would
make us all rambunctious, crossing paths and fighting for the last
available swing. Of course, we were kept on close watch for fear
that we would wander off into the woods or, worse yet, the street.
The staff at Clarke School worried about us getting on the street
because they knew that we wouldn't be able to hear a car coming.
So they had us clustered together like a troop of insects whenever we walked to class. If one of us strayed off the sidewalk, we

would receive a serious scolding. Discipline was what we needed to understand the importance of safety.

On weekends, only three of us remained at the school. As the only out-of-state girl in the entire dormitory, I had only the company of our caretakers and two boys: Peter from North Carolina and Mark from Pennsylvania. Only a small percentage of out-of-state students attended Clarke because of the money involved. Families of many students had moved to Massachusetts to take advantage of the free tuition, but many other students had been born in this state. My parents could have moved our whole family to Massachusetts, but Virginia was home with tons of relatives.

Miss Miller was clever to have the housemother take me, Peter, and Mark out of the classroom for a walk downtown so we wouldn't see parents pick up their in-state children for the weekend. It always worked because our heads were spinning with the excitement of having eaten ice cream or possessing a new wind-up toy when we returned to the dorm on Fridays in the late afternoon. The quietness of this dormitory didn't bother me too much, even though I sometimes felt lonely. Our small group could watch *Flipper* together and munch on popcorn.

My weekend stays at Leonard House didn't last too long, however. The parents of my classmate Cheryl Robbins began inviting me to their home in Greenfield, about twenty-five minutes north. Then the parents of my other good friend, Diane Karas, had me stay with them in Chicopee Falls, about twenty minutes south. These invitations were, at first, sporadic and then more frequent as those two families took turns hosting me every other weekend. Their hospitality would continue for seven years, which made my life at Clarke, a great distance from my family, so much easier.

I have cherished my wonderful friendships with Cheryl and Diane for nearly half a century. Our lives have all had a roller-coaster quality because of deafness. During our now rare visits, we have shared hearing-world dramas, laughed about old times at Clarke, and showered one another with great affection.

I flew home every six weeks, collecting about a hundred of airline pins in my lifetime. I do remember the thrill of coming home. Gazing from my seat out the window after the landing, my nerves would tingle all over at the sight of my entire family waiting at the outdoor gate. At that time, planes were not attached to telescoping corridors, so one could stand several yards from the plane. It was always a beautiful scene on a sunny day, all of my family and our black poodle Winnie clustered together. I loved that sight.

Despite seeing my family every six weeks or so, I was still tickled with their mail, especially a weekly Polaroid^{TM} picture of themselves waving to the camera, with "Hi Bainy" scrawled along the bottom white edge. One week I'd receive one of Mom and then another of Nash, each waving a hand, the same inscription on the edge. Sometimes the entire family was waving to the camera. It may sound a little goofy, but every Polaroid I received was a treasure for a lost little girl five states apart from her family.

Dad's mail was definitely my favorite. Every week I received his animal-photographed card with a drawn picture on the inside. His artistic talent and sense of humor were just magnificent. One in my memorabilia file says, "Your dumb old brothers are studying for the exams," with a drawing of a sleepy boy poring over his textbook while a log above him is being sawed. Another card reads, "We will find another way to get you home this Friday," accompanied by a drawing of a man riding on top of a big bird. All these hilarious pictures were neatly drawn with colored felt-tip pens and remain pristine forty-five years later. Most of all, I have been grateful for a father who knows how to express his love and affection with humor.

By now, after attending Clarke for a few months, I could now speak short, simple words with low-pitched sounds. One of my favorite words, I know, was "home" because I always associated it with a Polaroid of my family. Fortunately, this word was fairly easy for me to pronounce, although it took me a while to learn to say it. Miss Miller placed my hand in front of her mouth so I would feel her breath being expelled with the first consonant of "home" and then pressed my fingers against the side of her nose so I would feel the nasal quality of the M sound. To learn high-pitched consonants such as K and CH, Miss Miller held my hand in front of her mouth so I could feel the air or she had me watch a fluffy feather flutter as she made the sound. Too often, I was fascinated with the fluffy feather, not Miss Miller's mouth. I'm embarrassed to say she admitted to my unsurprised parents that my attention span was often short and that I was like "trying to pin down a butterfly."

Deaf children have to struggle to achieve not only the method of communication, oral or sign, but also language development. I would say even that it's much harder for them to learn to read and write than to learn to communicate. Hearing children, on the other hand, learn English or any foreign language spontaneously. It's easy for them to expand their language by listening to others speak, improving sentence structure, and using the right words. That advantage helps increase their ability to read and write, beginning with the kindergartner's attempt to associate written words with letter sounds.

With English or other spoken languages, deaf children have none of that. *They always have to be taught by someone.* That's why their English language development can take longer. In fact, it can take years for a deaf child to learn to write a flawless paragraph for an English paper. He or she is likely to use wrong words, run a sentence in disorder, or miss a necessary word. That's because the deaf child cannot hear others speak in sentences or is likely to misunderstand what is said. The important fact is that the ability to hear is the ability to read and write. Straight language and vocabulary are a never ending problem for all deaf children. The problem is not the learning disability deaf children have; it's just that they *miss out*.

Although our brains were perfectly normal, my classmates and I lacked straight language and, thus, were unable to learn a full sentence, while our hearing peers had already jumped to several levels ahead of us. Our teachers believed that, for us, the best approach for learning language would be, first, to identify an item and then to use verbs. Toward this end, we were to tackle two sets of index cards, one set consisting of nouns and the other of adjectives. We would have to learn to match cards from these two sets and place them under the right picture such as RED BOW or SAD CLOWN. We were learning language with our eyes.

The interesting fact is that deaf people are exceptionally keen with their eyes, able to detect the slightest movement several yards away. Because they have little or none of the auditory sense, deaf people treat their eyes as the number one sense for communication, education, security, and even entertainment. Deaf people are extremely visual. They "hear" with their eyes. They read speech. They read sign language. They read facial and body languages. They read TTYs. They read closed captions. They become alert to blinking lights of special devices. Deaf people are all eyes. That's how I feel about myself. I don't know what would happen if I lost my eyes. How on earth did Helen Keller get by?

That's why Miss Miller began our language education by teaching us to identify things—because of our visual awareness. We would easily learn that the long red strip tied into a knot was RED BOW and that the Bozo-like figure with his mouth arching downward was SAD CLOWN—if we got the adjective-noun order right. Then we would move on to the more difficult language pattern: verbs. We sure had a long, *long* way to go.

During my first two years at Leonard House, Diane Karas and Cheryl Robbins became my best friends. Their mothers had encouraged us to spend time together by inviting me to stay over for the weekends. Because I was with one or the other of their families every weekend, the three of us girls rarely spent weekends all together. Mrs. Karas told me she was saddened by the sight of me screaming in agony and running after my parents on my first day at Clarke. Diane had made numerous trips to Clarke before, so she wasn't at all upset when her mother left her. At that point, Mrs. Karas vowed to look after me. She sure did— for seven years. So did Cheryl's mother. I cannot thank them enough for making my life easier away from home.

Diane and her twin brother David are the youngest of five in the Karas family. David is not deaf because he wasn't affected by premature birth as his sister was. We still made a good trio, watching *The Brady Bunch* and playing board games; David treated us just the same. And I was enlightened with Mr. Karas's dry sense of humor as he constantly poked me in the tummy and teased about any sports team from my home state. A large man with a gentle heart, he certainly knew how to amuse small kids. Mrs. Karas spent a good deal of time boiling her famous Polish sausages. She even wrapped up one for me to take home to feed my family. In addition to being generous, she has always been a tough-talking, feisty lady who doesn't take rubbish from anybody. That's what made me admire her so much.

Cheryl has quite an interesting family because it has genetic tendencies toward deafness in it. She had a brother and two cousins attending Clarke at the same time. It was Cheryl's father who brought this gene to the family; he was mildly hard of hearing in one ear, but we considered him hearing for his normal speech. In fact, the deafness gene can be present but not active, and thus produce hearing babies. That's why Cheryl today has a deaf daughter and hearing twins. Those genes are unpredictable, continually creating surprises.

Me (on the left) with friends Diane and Cheryl.

Mrs. Robbins was, and still is, the easiest person to lipread on earth. She sure knows how to display the words she is saying on her lips. She could win a medal for that. I was secretly amused with her way of disciplining Cheryl. When exasperated with her daughter's misbehavior, Mrs. Robbins would say in a loud, clear voice, "Cheeerrruuuuuyllll!" Her lips would pucker up in a perfect *CH*; then her mouth would move into a neat wide arc for vowel sounds; and finally, her tongue would slap angrily against her front teeth for a perfect *L*.

My classmates and I had finally learned to say some complete sentences and could pronounce easy words without being misunderstood by strangers. Miss Miller had worked hard to drill language into our minds by making us read every sentence and by correcting our errors. From day one she and other teachers constantly said full sentences to us, knowing that we wouldn't be able to understand every word of them. They did it because they wanted us to catch a flicker of the language rhythm so we would learn that language did not consist of isolated words.

Small words such as *in, an,* or *the* pose a problem for most deaf people who lipread because these words are likely to be missed on the lips. They just whip by so fast that deaf people don't realize these words were ever said. I remember all the Clarke teachers trying to correct our sentences, reminding us not to forget those small, annoying words. Miss Miller had to keep reminding us to say "I have *a* black dog," not "I have black dog."

Despite having learned to use verbs, my classmates and I still lacked proper tenses. We would need more time to learn the difference between "am" and "will be." If you asked one of us, just an itsy-bitsy deaf kid, what we had for supper the night before and what we did afterwards, you would hear all the present verb tenses as if you were now watching the feast.

Every time I received mail from my family, Miss Miller read it out loud to me and explained the meaning of any word I didn't understand. When one of my brothers wrote about a baseball game, I didn't know what "by one point" or "home run" meant. I had no idea that language not only contained simple words with single definitions but also had word combinations and patterns that expressed various meanings. Like my classmates, I didn't know how complex language was.

It wouldn't be too long before my classmates and I advanced to the Lower School and finally learned to use proper verbs. Our English language development was just inching forward like the slow-turning pages of an unabridged Webster's dictionary. And, I was excited about moving to a new dormitory and about interacting with more kids my age. But I would hate to leave Miss Miller who was like a grandmother to me; she would remain the most favorite teacher of all my years at Clarke.

CHARLIE CHAPLINS

Clarke School organized its 200 students into four unique education levels according to chronological age, beginning with Preschool and ending with Upper School for students ages thirteen and up. Lower School was for those of ages six to eight; Middle School for those from nine to twelve. Most Upper School students graduated at the age of sixteen before joining ninth grade in regular school. Because of time-consuming oral education and slow language development, deaf children were likely to be a few years behind their hearing peers. I was now in Lower School, interacting with more kids my age and just taking time to learn.

Our new classroom was up on the second floor of Hubbard Hall, overlooking the hill down to Magna House where I was rooming with Cheryl and Diane. As we sat wearing headphones at our own desks, all arranged in a semicircular pattern, we took pity on the teacher's constant struggle with the microphone cord that tangled around her legs. Not a single day went by without someone tripping over the cord. Those cords were such a hassle that some teachers hung their mikes from the ceiling—a convenient solution, unless a very tall person walked by. BONK! With the overhead mike, one had to avoid making a painful mistake: Never let it go briskly or its elastic cord would spring, causing a smack on the head. Some deaf kids were mean enough to step on the cord behind the teacher and watch her snap back, arms flailing, and then say, "Oh, I'm sorry, I didn't see it."

I cannot remember if another favorite practical joke happened in my classroom, but I've heard stories about it many times. When the students entered the classroom, they had to remove their

hearing aids, put on the headphones, and adjust their volume
boxes. It was easy to do. After a while, they already knew what
level they would be comfortable with, even before hearing the
teacher's voice over the mike. Well, this time, when the teacher
finally spoke, the students yelped, peeling off their headphones
and commenting on how loud she was. Perplexed, the teacher
examined all the volume boxes and tried one of the headphones.
Then she pursed her lips in suspicion and demanded to know who
did it. It turned out that someone had sneaked in before class,
taken out all the knobs, turned the volumes way up, and put the
knobs back in to make them look like they were off.

Now that I could speak complete sentences, I could take
advantage of a new way to communicate long distance with my
family: a tape recorder, the old-fashioned type with reels. The
teacher directed me to hold a tiny mike and ramble on carefully
about what I had done over the previous weekend with either
Cheryl or Diane. If needed to, the teacher interrupted with her
corrections of my language, "Say 'I *went* to the circus last Saturday,'
not 'go.'" Then, before the three-inch reel was removed from the
recorder and sealed in an envelope to be sent off, I said good-bye
to my family.

Using their own tape recorder, my family responded with a
different reel that contained their voices. Listening to their tapes
was a thrill because they sounded like they were right behind me.
But I could hear only voices, not words. That's why the teacher
wrote down what the tape said and replayed it and ran her fingers
along the lines while my family spoke. With my headphone, I tried
to distinguish voices, which wasn't easy. Only Mom's voice was
recognizable because she was the only female. My brothers took
turns speaking into the mike, telling how much they missed me.

Mom and Dad flew up quite often and watched my class
before taking me, Cheryl, and Diane out for lunch. They had become immensely fond of my friends and sometimes met Cheryl's

or Diane's parents on campus and gave gifts to express their appreciation to them for looking after me on weekends.

Once, my three brothers came to visit me, and it was a nightmare for my mother. She ignored my dad's advice not to take all of those adolescent boys by herself, since he could not escape work to accompany her on a road trip to Clarke. Mom insisted on taking the boys for a cheery family adventure in spite of an absent father. Dad just sat back in a wait-and-see position at home and could not help smirking when Mom returned neurotic and wild-haired with a food-splattered station wagon and declared that she would never, *ever*, take all her kids on any trip without her husband again.

On that trip, Mom was mystified that my brothers were causing an uproar on campus, being chased by all the little Magna House girls. And sharing a hotel room with the three male adolescents rattled Mom. Nash refused to keep his radio down. Lindsay and Harvey constantly wrestled like a cat and dog. So Mom probably went through the whole trip without a single wink of sleep. She and the boys actually came up to bring me home for spring break, planning to take me out of there a day before all the other students departed. But the staff was concerned for the students' feelings and suggested that they wait until the last day to avoid hurt and jealousy. Well, after two days of dealing with the hype my brothers had caused on campus, the school president phoned Mom at the hotel and announced, trying to sound light and cheerful, "Bainy can go home a day early."

Clarke School was a strict school, demanding good manners, and when I came home, my parents were delighted to hear my polite words such as "Please" and "Thank you very much." But my formal manners made me seem stiff, set apart. And it wasn't only the manners that made me seem that way; it was also my using verbs in a formal way, along with my robotic voice. Because I couldn't hear backup conversation, I didn't know how to use informal verbs, some of which combined with pronouns, for example,

I'm and *won't*. Instead, I'd cautiously say "I am," "will not," and whatever was full and direct. In fact, that was how any eight-year-old Clarke student spoke. I'm sure all the teachers there would be mortified if we said "ain't" or "Nah" or "y'all."

Like most other deaf children, I had a flat voice that lacked accent and intonation. I sometimes talked through my nose, sounding as if I had a horrible cold. Even though I can pronounce some words just perfectly, my voice still sounds unnatural, like a strange foreign accent. It took me years to learn to speak with varying tones, and my voice is not as flat now as it used to be. Really, no severely or profoundly deaf person speaks in a natural voice, no matter how well he or she can pronounce words, even though the vocal cords are perfectly normal.

The reason we all have "deafy voices" is because we just don't know how to *monitor* our voices. We are unable to imitate sounds we cannot hear. We cannot hear our own voices as well as hearing people do. We just don't know how to make our voices rich with accent and intonation. That's why we are likely to talk flatly or very loudly. Every time my hearing husband Steve and I eat at a restaurant, I usually talk too loud because the surrounding sounds of waitresses clinking glasses or people yapping makes it hard for me to hear my own voice. Steve has to flap his hand down, lowering his gaze, and of course, I lower my voice. But then, I'm not sure if he can hear me okay. So Steve tells me where to stop the volume by quickly saying, "I can hear ya. Hold it right there." That's why I like a very, very quiet restaurant where I can tell whether my voice could wake the dead.

So you can see why it's difficult for most of us deaf people to have natural laughs. Yes, it's true that some of us laugh as if we are croaking or gagging. We just can't help that. Back in high school, one of my friends remarked that I never made any sound when laughing. So I asked Mom if she could teach me how to laugh. She looked at me aghast and said, "Huh? You laugh just fine. If you

smile, then people know you're amused." So I just left it at that
and continued laughing silently until after college, when I finally
quit worrying about what people thought of my voice. My laugh
isn't quite natural, but at least it feels good to let it all out. Over
the years, I've noticed that some of my deaf friends laugh silently.
I'm always touched to see people, hearing or deaf, smiling in spite
of this harsh world. The point is that deaf people are only hearing
impaired, not humor impaired.

During my third year at Clarke, I received the news that my former
teacher Miss Miller was "very sick"; at that time, I didn't know
what cancer was. She was diagnosed as having pancreatic cancer,
which wouldn't give her long to live. To my dismay, I noticed that
no one ever said she was going to get well. The teachers sure didn't
want to tell me it was a fatal disease, not to mention "cancer,"
because it would upset or confuse an eight-year-old. And I wasn't
old enough to understand that life could be so unpredictable.

One early morning, Miss Magner, an assistant to the school
president, picked me up, announcing that I would visit my old
teacher at the infirmary. At first I was excited, expecting to see
Miss Miller running after her fidgety students at Leonard House.
But Miss Magner knelt down in front of me with a grave look
and said, "She is still sick." Disappointed, I nodded and continued walking up the hill and across the campus, holding Miss
Magner's hand.

As we walked into a room at the infirmary, the bedridden
Miss Miller quickly held out her hand toward me—a powerful
memory I've had for the past forty years. Her pale arm stretched
out, her open hand waited to be clasped as if I was the life she
wanted to cling to. She was no longer a robust woman; she had
lost a great deal of weight. I moved to hold her thin hand and
chatted for a few moments, trying to boost her spirits with the
new words I could pronounce. Then Miss Miller said to me, "You

work hard for me. I want you to do well." I promised, accepting her hug. That was the last I saw of her. She died a few weeks later and I took it hard, but later, I became grateful for her happy, long life teaching deaf children to speak and read speech.

My friends and I had a variety of housemothers during our years at Clarke, one each year. About half of them were old and feeble, close to retiring; the other half were in their twenties and thirties and much more involved with us. One I remember the most: Miss Adams at Magna House. One evening, she taught me something about hearing people. For some reason, I wanted to get out of the playroom and asked her if I could go to the bathroom. She didn't believe me since we all just went after dinner. I crossed my legs in fake desperation, explaining that I had drunk an enormous glass of milk, and pleaded for her permission. After staring at me with a suspicious smirk, Miss Adams finally granted her permission, knowing very well what would happen. So she followed me to the bathroom and made me leave my stall door open, folding her arms. After pretending to do my business, I piped up, "Okay, I am finished." With a smug grin, Miss Adams said, "No, you're not. I would've *heard* it if you had gone to the bathroom. So you just stay and finish." Defeated, I sank further into the toilet, my butt nearly touching the clean water. That was the hard lesson I learned: *You can never fool hearing people when it comes to sound.*

Once, I received a brand-new raincoat from Mom through the mail, and I ached for rain on the spot. Cheryl and Diane, too, hoped it would rain and envisioned all three of us stomping through puddles, arms around each other. If we could, we would sing "Singin' in the Rain," but no. We would just skip around and giggle at each other. After hearing my pleading for rain all day, Miss Adams inhaled and said, "Okay, now I've heard enough about your raincoat. You should try what I tell you: Pray to God." I stared at her and then at Cheryl and Diane who shrugged as if to say that it might work. We found a corner to huddle, stood shoulder to shoulder, and clamped our closed hands together like a chorus of Christmas carolers. Then we prayed in our flat voices, "God, please make it rain tomorrow. Amen."

Lo and behold, it rained the next day. Cheryl, Diane, and I gaped at each other, standing before our bedroom window splattered with raindrops. Since that day, I have strongly believed in God and sometimes look at the ceiling in a fearful and apologetic way if I have done a bad sin. Although I was born Episcopalian, I went to Catholic mass every Sunday with either Cheryl's or Diane's families. Going to the services of a different religion never mattered to me because I was thinking only about God and Jesus. Besides, it was good to be with a family that I felt I belonged to. The Karases and the Robbinses never cared about my being a Protestant; they took me along, treating me like a family member.

Years later, I rediscovered something up in the attic and couldn't help chuckling. I had written a letter to God—not too long after the raincoat miracle, I remember. Mom was so touched that she saved it all these years. I now have the letter in my scrapbook. My handwriting in pencil looks pretty neat and bold with a lot of curves, not bad for an eight-year-old. But my language at that time wasn't perfect; the letter contains improper verb tenses, unnecessary words, missing words, and of course, a few misspellings. It reads:

Dear God,

    I am eight years old. I can not hear. I have a hearing aid. I love you because you are good and nice. I have three brothers! I do not have any sister. This morning my brothers are gone to school. I came to our bedroom. I said, "Oh, that's messy!" I cleaned our room. I told the truth! A long time ago I was bad girl! I was little girl. I bite Daddy's arm. My mother was very cross with me. NAUGTY! (There is a drawing of a mean-looking girl labeled "Bainy" biting an arm labeled "Daddy's arm.")

My daddy is going to the hospital because my daddy is doctor. My birthday is July 16. I was born in 1961. I like the beautiful earth! (An awkward drawing of the earth and the sun is placed here.) *I live in Norfolk, Va. It is beautiful outside. I am going to ride bicycle. It have two wheels. Can you really do everything? I wish I could to. My brothers' name are Lindsay, Harvey, and Nash. Nash is sixteen years old. Lindsay is fifteen years old. Harvey is thirteen years old. My dog's name is Romeo. Romeo, Pop, and Miss Miller died. Pop and Miss Miller are sick! Romeo did not watch the car. The car hit him. They went in Heaven. You live in the sky.* (A drawing of clouds sits here.) *I love you!*

Love, Bainy Bilisoly

Although Clarke was dead set against sign language, we communicated by waving our hands. They were just informal hand gestures that the staff knew were not official sign language. Out of laziness, we sometimes talked silently, only mouthing words, which just about drove the teachers up the wall. "Use your voice," one of them would wearily say to us. Who can blame them? We came up to Clarke to learn to use our voices; this wasn't a mime school. But still, my friends and I prided on our expertise at lipreading silent words.

Because most of us were profoundly deaf, we rarely called to each other, so we used many other ways of catching attention. Next to hand waving, the popular method was shoulder tapping. If you were in our playroom, you would've felt like you were in a room full of Charlie Chaplins. We didn't mind walking across the room just to tap a shoulder. We were tapped so many times that we could have developed permanent craters on our shoulders, like those the astronauts saw from one of the *Apollo* capsules.

The next way to get attention was foot stomping. This method created vibrations through the linoleum floor. The housemothers must have had their fill of our little hard-heeled oxford shoes hammering on the floor. Although she won't admit it today, Cheryl was the loudest of all. Even if she was sitting, she would stomp on the floor hard and fast like a jackhammer. Then there was another way to create vibration: table pounding. That drove the staff bananas, especially if we sat at the dining table. We would constantly hear "No pounding!," but would still clobber the table with our clenched fists, a sound even worse than a gavel.

One method involved no sound or vibration: paperball throwing. All we had to do was crunch a piece of paper and throw it at whomever we wanted to summon. Why worry about walking across the room when the paperball could hit someone's face with a painless thwonk?

And one attention-getting method we all hated to the core— having our chins grasped and turned toward the speaker, either gently or roughly. Every one of us found it so irritating that we would balk loudly and rub our chins in fake pain. We detested having our heads jerked around as though we were flimsy stuffed dolls that needed to be posed.

It's true that many small deaf children don't understand humor very well since they don't hear light teasing, jokes, or idioms in daily conversation. Although I learned early to laugh off fake comments concerning my appearance or even my mind, it was still difficult for me to pick up humor in conversation, even in college. Many of the jokes were hard to understand because they contained backup details that I had missed. So I just acted like a wallflower, grinning politely and silently. Wouldn't I look like an idiot if I were to let out a fake laugh, especially at the wrong time?

My dad's picture-drawn cards were the first to teach me about humor. When he wrote that he would get a big bird to fly me home, I laughed, knowing he was pulling my leg. Then it was my brother Harvey who taught me to laugh off fake negative comments. He has always been the nutty one in the family, drawing satirical faces and writing hilarious poems. My other two brothers, Nash and Lindsay, have never been without humor either. I must say that I come from a crazy family who, including Mom and Dad, know how to deal with sarcasm. We know how to prevent hurt feelings; we just don't pay attention to insulting comments.

Because we were not a perfect family, I did get hurt at times; however, I could see that my family hadn't meant to hurt me. They weren't always patient with me, and I did sometimes feel isolated from my family. It only happened when they were all yapping away during dinner, not acknowledging me. And it still does happen these days, so I haven't lost a sense of isolation.

It can be painfully difficult for hearing children to have a deaf sibling, especially if he or she is close in age. I have heard that many hearing children are jealous of how much attention their deaf siblings get from their parents. Well, of course, the deaf children need more attention in an *educational* way. It would be inexcusable if a deaf child received more love and affection than his or her hearing siblings. The hearing children also have to deal with the pain and embarrassment of having a deaf sibling, as they are likely to hear insults from other kids such as a neighborhood bully.

Because they were much older than me, my brothers didn't seem to have gone through many difficulties in having a deaf sister. The only time my brothers did fear embarrassment was when they had a girlfriend over. In truth, I was insulted by my brothers' fearful glances at me in the presence of their girlfriends, still, I understood that any teenager or college student would desperately try to impress a sweetheart with his "picture-perfect" family. But for the most part, my brothers have long treated me just the same, and we are still close these days.

As a sixteen-year-old, Nash was usually shy and spent a lot of time listening to the Beatles in his attic bedroom. In contrast to Harvey, he wasn't much of a talker or the wrestling type of brother. If his friends today are reading this book, I can imagine them dropping their jaws in disbelief because Nash is now known to be a garrulous attorney, full of snappy quips.

On a family vacation at the beach. From top to bottom: Nash, Harvey, Lindsay, my favorite cousin Kate Moring, and me.

Ever since he socked me in the arm to prove, erroneously, that I wouldn't cry, Lindsay has always been compassionate with me. When I was seven, he rode bikes with me to the neighborhood pool just to keep an eye on me. I remember once darting across the street and turning around to see Lindsay unmoved on his bike. When he slowly came up, I noticed tears running down his cheeks. To my chagrin, Lindsay explained that I would get hit by a car if I wasn't careful and reminded me that I couldn't hear. With a heartfelt embrace, I promised my fourteen-year-old brother I would stop and look both ways. Even today when riding the bike, I think about Lindsay's tears every time I prepare to cross the street. Always look both ways, period.

Mom and the seven other mothers of deaf children from the area went to the legislator in Richmond and urged that the state should pay for the tuition to schools for the deaf, no matter where the school was. After much deliberation, the legislator finally agreed to pay half of the tuition for out-of-state schools while planning new local programs such as mainstreaming. That marked the beginning of Public Law 94-142, the law that encouraged education of disabled students in the least restrictive environment. Today, this act is called the Individuals with Disabilities Education Act, or IDEA.

Because I had been at Clarke for four years and was doing well, my parents decided it was fair enough to pay half of the tuition instead of risking setbacks by transferring me to a school across the Chesapeake Bay that taught both oralism and sign language. I'm glad they decided to have me stay at Clarke because I had real friends there, especially Cheryl and Diane, and felt safe, even though I was way off in another state.

I continued to spend weekends with the Karases and the Robbinses. With the former family, I embarked on interesting adventures that I never had at home. Mr. Karas took us snowmobiling out at a cow farm that belonged to a friend. We rode through the open field at night, watching our headlights sail over the glittering snow. It was awesome. We milked the cows and struggled to aim the squirting white fluid into the bucket. And over at the Robbinses' I enjoyed other outdoor adventures, mostly ice-skating and camping. We slept in a tent and made S'mores over the fire by the river. Mr. Robbins, an avid outdoorsman, taught me, along with Cheryl and her brother Chuck, how to catch trout in the river.

Years later, Mom expressed her thought that these families had more influence on my life than my own family did. She was probably right. For a long time, I wondered how the Karases and the Robbinses managed to have another family's daughter over every other weekend, putting extra food on the table and buying an extra movie ticket. It was obvious that these families, in which both sets of parents had to work, were trying to make ends meet. One set had to handle two deaf children while the other set tried to support five children. But still those families treated me as if I were their own.

Vocabulary is indeed one of the biggest problems for deaf people. Hearing people learn new words every day by overhearing conversations or listening to them face to face; deaf people cannot. It's pretty much the same with writing. That's why it took me years to develop my English language to age level. When I learned a new word, I still had to learn how to use it. For instance, was that word a noun or an adjective? That's something I was not able to figure out spontaneously. Back then, I used to despise writing and was even afraid to write a personal letter for fear that I would construct a strange sentence or use words improperly. I was totally self-conscious with my insufficient language. But the shame went away when I started teaching myself to read and write in recent years, inventing my own methods. I believe any deaf person can do it, if motivated enough, and can learn to love writing as I do now.

After college, I stopped skimming through a novel or a newspaper and began to labor hard on the word-by-word method. Reluctantly, I became a slow reader, frequently going back to a sentence I didn't understand and trying to figure what it meant. Despite those time-consuming reading setbacks, I was delighted with my language expansion, which I pretty much attributed to my own efforts. I had been taught all my life, so it was time to motivate myself by reading.

If you asked me what I would consider to be the most important thing for deaf children, I would say literacy. I know the choice of communication and education methods comes first for a newly diagnosed deaf child because that choice will affect his or her whole life ahead. But then, regardless of the communication choice, a deaf child should learn to read and write English on his or her own. I strongly believe that literacy tremendously helps a deaf child become aware of the world, even if he or she is in the deaf community, which has its own language and culture.

At Clarke, we spent so much time on oral education and language development by blackboard that we weren't given a lot of reading material. I don't remember reading fables or any short classic novel. My classmates and I would've had a hard time understanding the novels of Laura Ingalls Wilder or Mark Twain. I'm not blaming Clarke for offering so little reading material; I understand that its main goal was to teach us to speak so we could be prepared to join the hearing world. What we were learning there was definitely time-consuming.

Diane and I had the same people in our class throughout the Middle School, although Cheryl had left to attend regular school. But her absence at Clarke never affected our friendship a bit because my weekend visits to Cheryl and her family continued. Every time she and her mother came to pick me up, I was full of questions about Cheryl's experiences with the hearing world. It also helped that her brother Chuck not only remained at Clarke but also lived in the same dorm; every time I passed him in the hall, I felt a strong presence of Cheryl and her famous foot stomping!

At Clarke, each class was limited to eight students because the smaller groups worked better for deaf children. Deaf schools typically don't allow large classes. How can a teacher get so many students to look directly at her lips or signing? My small class of children, all sharing the same disability, was a formative place for me and Diane to develop great friendships with those of the opposite sex. Just like any other preadolescent, I had a puppy love, stealing kisses behind the bush.

I even remember my first kiss. Lord, that happened in Miss Miller's class when I was just a tiny front-toothless pip-squeak. Chucky asked me if he could kiss me while Miss Miller was somewhere down the hall. I giggled with a nod. He leaned over and embraced me, kissing me on the lips. My body tingled with the sensation of his lips pressing on mine, although it lasted only for a second. I think even Miss Miller would have been touched at the sight of six-year-olds giving each other just one little smack on the lips and no more.

During my seventh year at Clarke, my parents met with the staff who suggested that they send me to regular school because my speech, though not always understandable, was good enough after years of oral education. But it was really because the staff feared that I was learning some of the official sign language, which was true. As we got older, my friends and I embedded some real signs in our usual informal hand-gesturing method. My parents were told that it could hurt my chance of functioning in the hearing world; therefore, it was time for me to go.

Mom and Dad decided to send me to a small private school five miles from our home. Knowing that it wasn't going to be easy for me, they discussed with the Clarke staff how to prepare me for a drastic change. They knew that, at first, it would be difficult for me academically *and* socially; therefore, I would need constant help with the homework and advice on how to make hearing friends.

I had mixed feelings about coming home for good. The good feeling was, of course, knowing that I would be with my family every day. The sad feeling was realizing that I would be leaving my deaf friends, especially Cheryl and Diane. Most of all, I was scared to death. How would I be able to interact with the hearing kids on a daily basis? I feared that my intelligence would be tested because I knew my language development was severely delayed. I was once at my hearing friend's house, peeking into her schoolbooks, and was amazed by the words I'd never heard of before. How would I be able to catch up with a hearing person, even if he or she were two years younger than me?

The plan was to make the transfer during spring break to give me more adjustment to regular school before starting afresh the following fall. I was to begin third grade despite my age—a few months before my twelfth birthday. Yes, that would put me three years behind. In fact, I had a vocabulary as scant as a kindergartner's. At that time, I had never heard of the word *transfer* or even *regular*. My deaf friends and I simply used the term *public school* and that was it.

The staff at Clarke began reminding me to use my voice and pay attention in class. I knew talking without a voice, like most of us did out of laziness, would be unthinkable with hearing kids. They wouldn't know how to lipread. And finally, the staff said I would have to work much harder than my hearing classmates to catch up, and I understood that completely. So I braced myself for the hard road to the hearing world.

ELBOW GREASE

Many of my friends have said that I have a keen memory of just about everything, and it may be true. March 1973 was when I began energizing my memory to a permanent hustle because it was the beginning of my dramatic years in the hearing world. Because of my deafness, I have relied on sight to keep memories, developing an enormous, sagging photo album inside my forehead. I can even feel its weight. Whenever I see something dramatic, *Click! Hold it right there,* and then this scene is remembered forever.

Emotion is the other way to keep my memories fresh. In the past, deafness had created an emotional roller coaster for me; I think I have experienced just about every single emotion you can imagine—fear, giddiness, anger, pleasure, sadness, joy, despair, and so on. In fact, this disability is extremely sensitive to emotion and to sight, and deaf people remember well by feeling and by picturing scenes.

When Mom dropped me off at Garrison-Williams School, the kids—more than a hundred of them, of all grades—started gawking and following me. I couldn't help feeling as if I were an alien. Overwhelmed by the attention, I quickened my pace toward my classroom. I wanted to be treated like a regular kid, but here, it was all a circus.

As I stood facing my new fellow third graders, a feeling of uneasiness swept over me. I was physically bigger than most of these eight- or nine-year-olds. I was on the brink of puberty, about to develop two bumps on my chest. I was the only hibiscus with crimped petals ready to blossom while my classmates were clamped-shut buds in the midst of large leaves. Towering over those classmates, I didn't, however, feel *mentally* bigger. I knew their language skills were more advanced than mine since I had read their welcome letters and even had to ask Mom for clarification.

I realized that my classmates had been waiting for me to say something, possibly wondering if I could really talk. I awkwardly looked around and said, "Well, where do I sit?" Then came all the little index fingers pointing to the desk in the front row. I was relieved when Miss Mountcastle, whom I had met the previous week, walked in with a smile toward me, and I sat in my new desk that had no volume box or headphone.

I was struck by how different this class was from those at Clarke. There were so many desks behind me, instead of in a semicircular pattern. I ached to turn around and see whether there was something sneaky going on. I figured I'd be placed in the front row for the rest of my life. As I expected, it didn't do any good to sit in the front row. It wouldn't help me to understand fully what a regular-class teacher had to say. I could understand only a few words here and there in the fast talking, although I could hear the teacher's voice well with my hearing aid. This was a regular class, and it'd be a waste of time if Miss Mountcastle spoke slowly for only the one deaf child. I certainly didn't want that; I wanted regular treatment.

From that day on I developed a habit of daydreaming, which would continue all the way to college. That's why I was never bored. Why worry about trying to piece together missing parts of the spoken lecture when I can pick up only a few scattered words? I highly recommend daydreaming if you've got nothing else to do; it's good for the brain cells to wander around in relaxation like visitors at a museum. Unless you don't know how to look attentive, no one will know that you've got Dali-like scenes in your mind.

People have asked me if I was in a mainstream program and the answer is no. Mainstream means inclusion of deaf children in regular schools that provide interpreters in classes and special classes on the side. I could have been mainstreamed, but my parents felt that a small private school, along with their involvement with my schoolwork, would be worth a try.

Every deaf child is different, regardless of the degree of hearing loss or level of intelligence. Some do well with mainstreaming; others don't. That method has an advantage of introducing the deaf student to hearing peers and encouraging his or her English language development. But it may also cause loneliness and isolation. Opponents perceive mainstreaming as a disaster for deaf children, who are often unable to learn the normal means of communication despite interpreters. Hence, mainstreaming is controversial.

I managed well without mainstreaming because of my family's tremendous support. They always looked over my shoulder to be sure I wasn't going to flunk a test or miss a deadline for a paper. So I was able to muddle through difficult years of normal education before receiving my college diploma. It was a long, grueling battle from the day I entered Garrison-Williams as the tallest and oldest third grader. But it was worth it.

I was delighted to have Lindsay at home during my difficult ordeal; he was the only brother there at that time. Harvey was at a boarding high school in Northern Virginia, and Nash was in California for his freshman year at Menlo Park. I knew I was naive, so I depended on Lindsay for his advice on developing a social life with my hearing peers, many of whom had never associated with a deaf person before.

I realized I had to try everything to be accepted. Trying was fiendishly hard work. I tried not to say or do outrageous things because I still had trouble understanding right from wrong. Admittedly I wasn't always very tactful. I did occasionally blurt out something that caused people's hair to stand on end. One time, late at night, when Mom's company had not yet left, I walked in and cheerfully said, "Oh, you're still here?" Fortunately, my parents were never angry with my tactlessness; instead, they would outright tell me why it was wrong to say this or that.

I tried not to embarrass friends if I was tagging along with them nor my brothers when they had their girlfriends over at the house. More important, I tried not to embarrass myself. I constantly worried about whether my verbal remarks or actions would repel people. I had to rely on facial language to tell what people were really thinking. If I could have heard comments such as "You wouldn't believe what he said to her . . .," I would have been able to learn morality in a snap.

I also tried not to interrupt conversation. Even at a young age I knew deaf children had a tendency to do so. But it was difficult *not* to cut in because some people talked so low or moved their lips so slightly that I may have thought no one was talking. That often happened in a group. If I wanted to say something, I had to look around for unmoving lips before jumping in.

When I was in a conversation with a group of friends, I tried to look included even though I could not decipher the swarm of words flying around. I tried not to look frustrated because I didn't want people to feel sorry for me. I just pretended to listen, my eyes secretly darting around for body language. The hardest part of a group conversation was when everyone suddenly erupted into laughter; I didn't want to be the only one not laughing. Therefore, I felt compelled to let out a fake laugh, which made me feel like an idiot. But I figured that laughing along with the group made me look included.

Despite the feeling of isolation, I was determined not to let group conversation bother me too much. It was something I knew I would have to face for the rest of my life, and I had long gotten used to missing conversation. I never wanted people to feel sorry for me. But now, in the hearing world, I began hearing pitying remarks about my deafness as if it were a death in the family. Inwardly annoyed, I responded by shrugging it off to indicate that deafness was not a tragic thing.

Now that I was dealing with hearing peers on a daily basis, I would have to try with all my resourcefulness to be accepted. I envisioned a long winding road with fallen rocks here and there ahead. With this rough disability, I'd likely either skip around or smash into obstacles, possibly more of the latter. That road was not going to be smooth at all.

I didn't do too well in third grade because of my limited language. All the technical words in the textbooks threw me off, and I had to turn to my parents for help. With her history degree, Mom took delight in teaching me about immigration during the early 1900s. And Dad prided himself in explaining photosynthesis to me, holding up a camellia leaf he had plucked from the yard. Of course, he left out the chemicals such as CO_2 (carbon dioxide) and O (oxygen) and only said, "The sun goes inside and that's what makes the leaf breathe."

My parents and the school staff decided to move me up to fifth grade the following fall so I'd be with those closer to my age. I remember taking a literacy test at the end of school year, and I don't think I even passed it. But that didn't prevent my parents from deciding to let me skip fourth grade; they assumed I'd eventually pull through under their close surveillance.

Fifth grade was even harder because I went through a bad phase. I had befriended a girl who taught me to behave like a bully, picking on weaker girls. That's why I became difficult at school—just temporarily. I do feel bad thinking about it, but I have apologized to those I hurt. Without realizing it, I had become good friends with the wrong person. I just thought M.J.'s tough attitude was cool, and I was willing to do anything to please her.

Now that memory is hard for me to share. But I want to remind you that it's difficult for a deaf child to understand right from wrong. Some hearing kids know this and take advantage of it. I've heard stories about deaf children being guided into doing something outrageous by their hearing peers who tell them there is nothing wrong with it. Then the hearing kids get a thrill of watching deaf children discredit themselves. That's what M.J. did to me. She told me to strip in front of the neighborhood boys, promising that they would become enamored with me. And I did. That's the truth. I took off all of my clothes, from head to toe. I kept on doing it because M.J. egged me on, praising me and calling me her best friend. Deep down in my heart I didn't feel comfortable stripping, but all I wanted was to be accepted.

She also taught me to bully my own classmates, saying it was cool to push them down on the ground or knock their books off the desks. And I believed her. The school staff was obviously reluctant to tell my parents how difficult I had become, so Mom and Dad never knew I was going around shoving people down, using bad words, or being rude to my teacher.

There was another reason for my toughness: I wanted to hide my vulnerability as a deaf girl in the hearing world. I remember pushing a small girl down on the ground and then feeling my heart wrench with shame. I didn't feel good about what I did. This girl hadn't done anything to me. But in a selfish way, I was more concerned about looking tough to mask an extremely sensitive disability.

When we rode our bikes to a grocery store, M.J. goaded me into stealing a pack of cigarettes, emphasizing the word *sneak* and even demonstrating how to tiptoe. Did she secretly want me to get caught—just to see the excitement of handcuffs slapping over my wrists? For the first time, I questioned our friendship, staring at M.J.'s wicked grin. But I was still too intimidated by her dominance. So I reluctantly went into the store, slipped Marlboros into my coat pocket, and casually walked out. No, I didn't feel good about stealing; I knew it was wrong.

After that, I wanted to get away from M.J. but didn't have the courage or didn't know how. I was all alone and confused with the trap I was in. As I grew to realize, M.J. was not a real friend. But I didn't know what to do and was afraid to turn to somebody for help. I feared that M.J. would retaliate if I told her that our friendship was kaput.

Luckily, the other two girls in the neighborhood pulled me out of the entanglement. I remember that corner of the street where those girls, Ashby and Anne, summoned me. They stood so close together with anxious looks that I knew they had rehearsed for this encounter, something unusual for eleven-year-olds. Finally, they declared to me in an alternate fashion, "What happened to you? You've turned mean. You used to be a nice girl but M.J. has changed you. And you're getting a bad reputation. You need to get away from M.J." After listening in shame, I thanked Ashby and Anne for their concern and promised to do better.

I walked home, upset and unsure how I would get out. Then a solution entered my mind, and I hesitated, pushing it off and then pulling it back in. It was going to be a huge risk, but I'd do it to get away from M.J. So I approached my mother after dinner when she was preparing to take a bath. I asked if we could talk, uncomfortably looking at her long green velvet bathrobe. Mom sensed something was wrong and had me sit down on the edge of her bathtub. Then she listened to me confess about smoking and pushing down people. I told her it was M.J. that guided me into it. Because I was too ashamed, I didn't tell her about stripping. So I stopped the confession right there and fearfully waited for her reaction. This solution was now started but not yet completely done, as I expected. Shell-shocked, Mom stood up and walked around. She then disappeared without a word. I just waited on the edge of the bathtub, my nerves all shot.

Dad barged in, ranting and raving, and it surprised me because he was normally a laid-back person. While Mom stood by in a daze, he slumped down and stared at me in disbelief, which caused my eyes to water. I told him I was sorry and would never do that again. It took my parents several moments to calm down and declare that I was strictly forbidden to see M.J. That's exactly what I was aiming for. I needed my parents to help bring me out of the mess. Fortunately, they didn't ground me because I agreed to stop hanging around with M.J.

M.J. was baffled when I told her I could no longer see her. I lied that my parents had found a cigarette in my coat pocket right after I left her house. Just a little white lie to get myself out of her retaliation. And it worked. I'm glad I confessed to my parents because it made me a nice girl again. Up to this date I've always been very grateful to Ashby and Anne for opening my eyes. Although it pains me to remember this bad phase, especially stripping and all, I don't feel anger toward M.J. because she was just so undisciplined. As long as my life has turned out well in spite of painful past experiences, there is no reason to hate someone who had treated me badly. Those who are cruel definitely have a problem and need help.

It had been two years since I entered the hearing world, and my grades had improved tenfold with the advantage of a small class of ten or fifteen. My classmates were kind enough to tell me what page to look up or what book to pull out from under my desk. As always, I sat in the front row but still daydreamed while trying to look attentive. What did I daydream about? No telling.

My language development, though still several years behind, had grown steadily in the hearing culture. When I first heard, "a substitute teacher" at school, I waited until I got home to ask Mom if she would spell out the first word for me. Normally for deaf people, it's hard to learn a new word just by lipreading because not all consonants can be heard. That's why I started to concentrate hard on reading. But the problem was, whenever I came across a new word and learned its meaning, I wondered how to pronounce it. So it turned out that I had to learn vocabulary both ways, by reading and oral methods.

I felt accepted by hearing friends who eventually grew to understand my deafness. They treated me like a regular kid, trying to compete with me in running relay races or shooting ball. I had made the school basketball team, and Max the coach invented hand signals for me to read across the court because it wouldn't be a good idea to try to read lips while I was running. I'd end up plowing into other players or smashing into the padded wall like a housefly.

I was invited to slumber parties, where I learned that hearing kids in a gathering don't ever fall asleep once the lights are turned out. They just keep yapping away no matter how sleepy they are. Well, I guess it's more of a comfort for hearing people to talk in the dark. For deaf people? Forget it; they would rather snooze than struggle to lipread or sign in the blackened atmosphere. Whenever I was slumbering with those friends, I could tell if gossip or jokes were tossed back and forth, although I had removed my hearing aid and heard absolutely nothing. I could see the small hand gestures or feel the one next to me shaking the floor with her laughter.

Now that I was a teenager and becoming more concerned with vanity, it was time to get the behind-the-ear hearing aids. The old hearing aid I had had for years was about to conk out. I was sad about giving it up because it had brought all those first pleasant sounds to my ears. But I wouldn't miss those straps or protruding earpieces that stuck out like corks or those twisted cords that sometimes got caught in a tree branch, yanking off one of my earpieces. When I entered the hearing world, I cut the torso straps, leaving only the one around my neck. I wore my hearing aid like a necklace inside my shirt and that provided comfort. But the trouble was that, whenever I ran down the basketball court, it looked as though I had an abnormally large heart beating violently through my chest. I'm sure it scared the dickens out of the opponents because they didn't know what the heck was thrashing around inside me. I began to tuck the front strap behind my teeny-weeny bra and it helped, though not perfectly.

Mom and I flew to Clarke to receive my new hearing aids, which I could have gotten locally, but this school understood my hearing loss better and would select the right brand for me. I was overwhelmed to be back on this unchanged campus after two years. Diane was delighted to see me, nearly knocking me down with her embrace. To my astonishment, she had shot up several inches above me. So had Cheryl and all the old friends. It was weird how fast adolescents could grow in a short period of time.

Meeting with the school audiologist, I was tickled to once again take hearing tests, which I had done every year at Clarke. The fun thing about hearing tests is that they challenge you, like a game of musical chairs, to catch the lowest sound by raising your hand exactly at the right time. Although I could see the audiologist's face through the tinted glass window between us, I could not see his hands as he manipulated the audiometer, sporadically sending various tones to my headphones. As I attempted to figure out whether I was hearing an actual sound through my headphone or just an echoing in my head, I must have raised my hand a hundred times when there was no actual sound at all! The hearing test found that my hearing loss had remained the same as several years before, about a 75 percent loss in both ears. The audiologist then decided on the right kind of hearing aid for me.

I don't remember whether I had earmolds made there or somewhere else ahead of time. In fact, it takes an earmold a few days to harden. The earmold-making process is the most icky part of the whole thing. Imagine sitting there while a big fat syringe injects soft pink material into your ear and you suddenly feel it swish inside like mousse. It tickles, for sure, especially if that foam is cold. When the audiologist yanks it out, it looks like strawberry meringue.

They fit so well, that I knew it would take time to remember that I had these behind-the-ear aids on; I was so unaware of them that I would accidentally crash into bed with them on—and worse yet, dive into the pool, which I did once that year. Hearing aids can be unpredictable, no matter what type they are. I've heard about some hearing aids being ruined simply because of a small splash of water. Yet my audiologist told me a strange story of an old man who forgot about his aid in his pants pocket and threw these pants in a washing machine. Even after being flounced around in soapy water, the man's aid turned out fine. Don't ask me how it survived.

I was thankful for the trip all the way up to Massachusetts, and it was a memorable one because I had a chance to reunite with the Karases and the Robbinses at the former's house where we feasted on Mrs. Karas' Polish sausage. This trip also gave me a unique bond with Mom because she perfectly understood how much a visit to the "old world" meant to me.

But traveling wasn't always so comfortable. Whenever I reminisce about one incident that nearly put me in danger, I shudder and quietly scoff at my own dumb mistake. I made a mistake and never did it again. Mom and I were in New York City with my grandmother Donnie for the Bicentennial celebration. After spending a spectacular Fourth of July on the harbor, we retreated to our hotel dining room where we had dinner and chatted with our waiter. In truth, I thought he was a nice-looking guy with gracious manners. The next day, I happened to run into him in front of the hotel while Mom and Donnie were still packing in their room. He asked if I wanted to get in a taxi with him for a ride and said something I didn't understand but I just let it go and told him I had twenty minutes.

So yes, I did get in the taxi with the waiter, someone I hardly knew anything about. But he seemed gentle and friendly. As long as we were in a public place with the cabbie, I thought it would be safe to ride along. If this waiter had his own car, I would have said no. When I was seven, my family warned me not to get in a car with a stranger. My brothers kept asking me the same question over and over, "What do you say when a man offers you candy and asks you to get in his car?" After hearing this so many times, I learned to say a firm "No."

Now I was sitting in the back seat with the waiter, zooming down Park Avenue. Just then I began to feel uncertain and asked the waiter where we were going. To my dismay, he responded that we were going to a movie. Since it was broad daylight, I immediately knew something was fishy. My body tensed when the waiter put his hand on my knee. I inwardly panicked when we parked in front of a seedy movie theater with weird names. The waiter held out his hand to help me out of the car but I sat there paralyzed. Finally I told the cabbie to take me back to the hotel pronto. Luckily the waiter didn't protest and rode on without a word.

To my great relief, we ended up at the hotel again, and I quickly climbed out of the taxi, leaving the waiter. After it drove on out of my sight, I stopped in my tracks and tightly shut my eyes in shame. Why did I do this? I asked myself in a silent shout, clenching my fists. When I hesitantly entered the lobby and saw my mom at the checkout counter, my heart sank as I realized how close I had come to putting my family in agony. Mom turned to me with a pleasant grin, and her unknowing look made me want to hug her. I couldn't hold it in and told her what happened. Mom stared at me incredulously and exclaimed her words that pushed me into further shame: "You're *fifteen*! How could you do this?!"

Visibly shaken, Mom and Donnie barraged me with questions and asked why I got into the car with someone I barely knew, especially in *New York City.* I explained that they, too, thought the waiter was super friendly from the night before. Mom protested that he was still a stranger and that we knew nothing about him other than he waited tables. The whole incident was a hard lesson for me and made me more cautious with strangers, even the friendly ones.

Years later, I babysat my brother Nash's dog at my house, playing ball with her in the front yard. A little girl rode by on her bike and stopped to ask if she could pat Molly the dog. After hearing my resounding "Yes," the girl played with the dog and chatted with me for about a half hour. Well, a few weeks later, the same girl pedaled by and I approached, asking if she would like to see my fish pond. The girl thrust her hand at arm's length and said in her outright tone, "No, I don't know you." It was like a slap in my face, but I was intrigued by how a five-year-old girl could protect herself. She then looked at me in half-recognition and asked if I had a white dog named Molly. After I answered yes, the girl demanded to see my fish pond. As we walked to the back yard, I praised her for giving me that kind of response. The girl continued to come by to feed the fish and chat with me before moving away to another city.

Ever since the encounter with this five-year-old girl, I have been amazed by how quickly small hearing kids can learn to avoid danger by listening to warnings. I understand it takes time and effort to warn any small child to shun a "friendly man" who offers candy or asks for help finding his lost puppy. I cannot help feeling anxious about deaf children who are not able to learn safety the same way hearing kids do, at least, possibly not as fast as they need to. The point is, deaf children are able- bodied and can run loose like hearing kids; however, they may be deprived of these important warnings. Just as deaf children have to practice new words over and over, they need to be warned many times about the same thing.

I went to Old Dominion University once a week for my language sessions and learned that people used clichés in their language. When I first heard "paint the town red," I imagined people marching down the street with buckets of red paint and splashing it over everything in sight—trees, buildings, traffic lights, you name it. But then I learned it meant to celebrate. With his laid-back humor, Dad explained what "bite the bullet" and "foot in the mouth" meant.

In college, I still felt that I had missed a lot of this humorous type of language and purchased *The Dictionary of Clichés*. Even today, I still have to grapple with some of the meanings. While my mother-in-law was housesitting for us, she cleaned the bottom of our shower, removing the gray coating which I had tried to do many times without luck. Well, when we came home and saw the immaculate bottom in our shower, I called my mother-in-law to ask how on earth she did it. She chuckled and replied, "Elbow grease." I paused, picturing a clear plastic bottle with yellow fluid in it. Then came my naive question, "Where did you get it?"

My parents would not allow me to withdraw throughout the entire dinner without saying a word. They were trying to encourage me, as a teenager, to be a better conversationalist. The truth is, I was not as explicit as I should have been. I always gave too short an answer such as "Yes" or "It was fine." Actually I could've rattled on with interesting details if I had heard how people answered questions. No wonder Mom and Dad constantly urged me to "tell more about it." They also tried to boost the way I answered questions or reacted verbally; they taught me how to speak in spirited tones. I remember Mom urging me to say "Ssshhuuuruh!" instead of a flat "Sure." In fact, my deafness had deprived me of expressive language.

Over the years, people had often waited for my reaction, perhaps wondering, "Don't you appreciate what I've just said?" I could see that my lack of response peeved some people, making them think that I was unfeeling. Their perceptions did worry me, but I was more scared of blurting out wrong words. I desperately fumbled for the right words to express my feelings before it was too late. It took me several years to be more verbally expressive. Eventually, I learned the proper words to show my feelings and ways to fluctuate the tones of my voice.

I realized that people spoke differently even though they spoke the same English language. I came home from Clarke, proud of my oral accomplishments but, then, was baffled at the way people here in Virginia talked differently from those up north. Many people here pronounced "house" as "hose" instead of opening their mouths into an "ow" shape as I had seen on northerners. Whenever these people said, "Come by to my house," I wondered if they were asking for help to water their plants? It took me a while to accept the southern accent. And I'd keep the northern accent Clarke had taught me—no sense in turning my expensive oral skills into effortless, tongue-loosening drawls. So these days, I seem to be the only one in the family who pronounces "to-MAY-toe" while everyone drawls "tuh-MAWH-toh."

Regardless of accent, everyone has different lip movements. Some talk from one corner of the mouth, and others move their lips as if they are chewing hard caramel apples. I don't mean to sound critical, but it galls me when someone talks way too forcefully, spraying saliva. As my stomach turns, I try desperately hard not to distort my face. It's nerve-racking when that person begins each word with a *T* or a *P*, propelling a tiny droplet in slow motion toward my face. I scream in my mind, *Yaaaaah!*, before it hits me in the corner of my eye or on the tip of my nose. Of course, I fight the powerful urge to wipe my face because I don't want to hurt feelings. But once I'm alone, I rub my entire face like mad or even throw water on it.

FRAGILE LEAF

As I had hoped, nobody followed me on the first day I entered Norfolk Collegiate School as a ninth grader. Everyone wove their way through the halls, apparently indifferent about having a deaf girl among them. Fortunately I had already gotten to know many of the people who attended this small private high school, particularly, those who, like me, had gone to basketball camp there during the summer. After having played basketball for Garrison-Williams, I made the junior varsity team in no time. Sports was where I felt readily accepted in the hearing world and where I could prove that deafness did not limit athleticism. That's why I intentionally played sports throughout high school, ending up with tennis as my favorite sport. My efforts in sports would help me achieve the true double-A rating: able-bodied and ambitious.

Still, I did make one sports blunder. It happened when we switched ends of the basketball court after halftime. In the third quarter, I kept forgetting that we were supposed to score at the other end. You guessed it, when I had the ball, I scored for the other team. Proud of my scoring, I spun around only to have my ego deflate at the sight of everyone at the other end. If I had been able to hear my teammates yell for me to come back, I would have turned around. I had seen hearing players head the wrong way, too, but they were saved by the verbal alarm behind them.

I was still the oldest in my class, two years behind, but I considered these kids my age anyhow—except for one huge point: I could drive and they couldn't. They had just entered puberty, and I had just gotten my first driver's license. So I drove my friends to the mall and wherever ninth graders liked to hang around; that made me feel important, not used. Besides, I wanted to get out of the house on weekend nights.

I've been told that deaf people make the best drivers because they tend to be more attentive to the road for fear of colliding with an ambulance. I do get jittery about missing a warning sound, but my strong hearing aids enable me to hear a low-pitched car horn or even swear words. I don't blame those whose hearing cannot be helped by amplification for being scared of ambulances. But I have not heard of many accidents involving deaf people and emergency vehicles. Apparently, deaf people are able to detect a tiny red blinking light in a heartbeat.

Anyway, I'm not a bad driver, but when I have a passenger with me, well, that can be risky, particularly because I have to swing my eyes back and forth as I watch my friend's lips and the road. Fortunately, this distraction has not caused me to have a wreck. Diane once picked me up at the Hartford Airport in her Lincoln as huge as a Russian tank. I suggested that we, as hard of hearing people, shouldn't chat during the half-hour ride to her house, especially in a car that big. Diane dismissed it with a wave of her hand. Anyhow, we did talk nonstop the whole way while she managed to move her neck every two or three seconds, not once weaving on Interstate 91.

I can imagine how hard it is to sign while driving, but again, I believe deaf people have an ability to avoid accidents. I was once in a car with the three signing girls and it turned out fine, although the car did weave a little. I watched the driver briefly steer the wheel with her knee if she had to sign with both hands. She was driving well below the speed limit, which may have helped to keep everyone safe and happy.

When I started driving, Mom had to keep reminding me to turn off the blinker because I couldn't hear its clicking noise. Poor Mom, with her perfect hearing, had to listen to it for a very long time when I was a nervous, inexperienced driver who thought it was necessary to turn on the blinker at least a quarter mile before making the turn.

I've had a minor car accident attributed to my deafness, and luckily, no one was hurt. It was rainy and foggy, so all the windows were hard to see through. Trying to get on the road from a convenience store, I asked my two friends sitting in front to look to the right and see if it was clear to go. They both yelled "No!" but I plunged ahead—and rammed an old Mustang broadside, causing $500 worth of damages. Why did I accelerate instead of wait? I thought my friends said, "Go!" Ever since then, I've tried hard to distinguish between "No!" and "Go!" but I tell people they'll have to either shake a head or wave me forward with a hand.

I had become good friends with Elizabeth Forsberg, and when I first met her in fifth grade, I was touched by her curiosity about my deafness. Always full of pep, Elizabeth asked all kinds of questions such as how much I could hear with my aid. The more she learned, the more she helped. That's why we have remained close all these years, although she now lives a thousand miles away. I will never forget one big lesson Elizabeth learned about deafness when we were looking for homecoming dresses at the mall.

While we browsed in an apparel store, an eager salesgirl asked me to try on a dress she found. So she and Elizabeth waited while I was trying it on in a curtain-drawn room. What I didn't know was that the salesgirl kept asking me questions and waited for me to answer. "How does it fit?" No response. "Ma'am? The dress? Is it okay?" Silence. "Hello? Um...how about the dress?" Nothing. All this happened while my idiot friend stood there without a single word, her cheeks puffing out to keep from laughing. She even shrugged when the baffled salesgirl asked her why on earth I had not said anything.

After we left the store with my new dress, Elizabeth told me what happened. Aghast, I asked her why she didn't tell the salesgirl about my deafness. Her answer came out in a pitiful way: "I didn't want to embarrass you." Just then I gave Elizabeth a lecture about how it would be even more embarrassing if people didn't know about my deafness and that she should inform them right away. As she listened, Elizabeth tucked her head with a tiny smirk. Oh, how I wish I had seen that salesgirl talking to a curtain; that would have been great entertainment!

Like a typical high school kid who dated, I went to formal dances and informal parties, and it was in those settings that I realized with dismay that a loud atmosphere would always make it impossible for me not only to hear but also to be heard. To hear in those settings was, and is, much easier because I could still lipread and understand what people were saying. To be heard in those settings was impossible. I couldn't make myself loud enough, even if I was screaming from the top of my lungs. Because I couldn't hear my own voice in the earsplitting environment, I just didn't know how to monitor it. In addition, projecting my voice at the highest volume distorted my words. People had to lean over to understand what I was saying, but it didn't help, so they just gave up and turned to somebody else. It still happens these days; however, I manage to avoid loud parties. I do like to socialize, seeing old and new friends all together, but only if it's a cocktail party, cookout, or wedding. In recent years, I've come up with a solution to converse with somebody in a loud atmosphere: I suggest that we move to another room or a quiet corner. A friend has no objection to it.

Diane was about to graduate from Clarke after spending twelve years there, and I flew up there to attend the ceremony as well as spend time with my old surrogate families. I met Cheryl's hearing friends at her school picnic and noticed that she interacted with the hearing peers the same way I did, friendly but careful not to offend. Because Cheryl's friends were a group of unknown kids,

I was awfully shy around them. Cheryl didn't seem that way with her friends, constantly asking what was going on. But the funny thing is, when Cheryl and her family visited me a year later, I took her to a friend's house where many girls gathered, and she was so shy that she never said a single word. Our circumstances and behavior had completely reversed!

When I reunited with Diane at the graduation ceremony, I wondered how she'd be able to handle the hearing world after spending so many years in special education. I feared that the change was going to be much too drastic a change for Diane as a sixteen-year-old. However, I managed to keep these feelings to myself and gave her my congratulatory support. Then I stayed with her at the family cottage on the lake. Laura, another Clarke student who had graduated with Diane and who was also my roommate long ago, lived close by, so we walked over there a lot. I admit it, the whole visit was awkward, but not because of the Karases. It was because of *friends*. Diane and I were at an age where we struggled to fit in. I could see that Diane was anxious to keep up with Laura and other deaf friends despite the fact that they would now go to separate schools.

When we sat in Laura's den facing the lake, I couldn't escape the feeling of isolation. Yes, they were the same friends I had at Clarke, with whom I had once felt comfortable and happy. But it had been five years since I left them, so I felt more immersed in the hearing world in spite of its obstacles. I should've been more delighted to be with friends of the old world but I was sixteen, a young emotionally immature sixteen, and had a serious boyfriend constantly on my mind. And I worried about who my friends were.

I struck up a conversation in a lighthearted way to break the ice and used some of the old hand signals, fondly remembering how we communicated in the past. To my chagrin, they looked at me weird and then questioningly at Diane who didn't say anything. As I sat there embarrassed, I realized that these hand signals were a thing of the past, now considered "baby talk." I got up to go to the bathroom just to escape the tension. Worse yet, I felt isolated from Diane, my old best friend, and she seemed to feel the same way about me.

On the way home I was disheartened at the possibility of drifting away from Diane. But then her letter came. Diane wrote like she did before, describing her summer activities, and asked *twice* if I had a good time. It was a worried question. Obviously, she didn't want to drift away either. Wanting to be an honest friend, I wrote Diane back and explained why I felt uncomfortable with the deaf friends after spending five years in the hearing world. I also wrote of my desire to keep our friendship intact, no matter what. Diane responded with understanding and promised to keep me posted on how she was faring in regular school. Needless to say, I knew that her first entry into the hearing world would start out overwhelming and painful. So I prayed hard that she would be able to handle it okay.

Social life was becoming more difficult for me. My friends and I had outgrown neighborhood activities such as climbing trees. Our bodies had reached full adolescence, and our energy levels had become more passive, except when we engaged in sports. We were now mid-teenagers who cherished only a few activities, one of which was to sit around and talk. Talk, talk, talk—imagine how hard it was for a deaf teenager in the hearing world. Of course, I hated it, but there was nothing I could do about it, and I kept quiet, seething inside.

I remember tearfully complaining to Mom that I felt like everyone was ignoring me. With a heartfelt embrace, she explained that they may have not intended to because I was usually so quiet that they forgot I was there. Mom was probably right, but in a group of less than three girls, well, I wouldn't think so. Not everyone was patient enough to talk slowly to me; they could manage only to say "Hi" with a quick grin before walking away.

For anyone, growing up involves pain. Everyone tries to fit in, and self-esteem quivers like a fragile leaf, going up and down and sideways—the movement of insecurity. I had seen in high school that teenagers do a lot of backstabbing. Even good friends backstab one another. Whispering and snickering negative things behind backs are even more hurtful than a knife; the cruel words you hear (if by unfortunate chance) can creep to every part of your body and linger there longer than a flesh wound.

The threat of backstabbing had me worried all the time, paranoid. I couldn't hear what people said behind me, and I kept thinking they were talking about me. Maybe they were. Maybe they weren't. All the way through high school and college I became testy whenever people walked or stood behind my back. The paranoid feeling was difficult to avoid. My psychologist friend has told me that foreigners who know little or none of the English language react the same way. As a matter of fact, deaf people and foreigners are very much alike, both having to learn the language and not understanding the jabbering around them.

My teenage phase wasn't horrible; it had its normal ups and downs. I did make wonderful friends who have stuck with me to this day. Back then, they helped tremendously, letting me copy their school notes and explaining what went on in the movie we had just seen. But I have to admit that my friendship with them wasn't the confiding type because I built a wall around myself, not expressing my feelings in the hearing world to anyone. Because I didn't want sympathy, I harbored the occasional blues, put up a smiling face, and pretended to blend with the hearing world while there was an invisible wall around me.

At the time of my eighteenth birthday I flew up to Clarke for two weeks of speech therapy, and it was indeed productive. Beth the therapist and I worked for a couple hours twice daily, and each time was like military training. If you spend two hours repeatedly coordinating the movements of your tongue, lips, cheeks, and jaws for just one word, you will just about crash. Your brain will seem to weigh a ton from the intense concentration on making perfect vowels and consonants. Sure enough, I was dead to the world by the end of each session, my jaws aching like crazy, but I managed to bounce back after lunch or a good night's sleep.

I had developed a habit of talking through my unmoving jaw since attending regular school. After years of communicating with deaf friends, I began to realize that I didn't have to talk slowly and deliberately around hearing people. Hence, I relaxed my mouth just a bit too much, not bothering to move my jaws wide enough as I tried to talk like a hearing person. Eventually, I was often running my sentences in a blur, all through my unmoving jaw. No wonder people asked if I had broken my jaw. I needed to learn to articulate the vowels coming out of my mouth. If I said, "Bob," it sounded like "Beb," with my mouth hardly moving a centimeter. This intensive speech therapy was providing a challenging work-out for my jaw muscles that had gotten so far out of shape!

I also learned of my other speech impediments; one was the way I held my breath until I finished talking, letting out excess breath at the end of the sentence. When Beth told me what I was doing, it certainly didn't sound like an attractive speaking style. Beth taught me to inhale before talking and exhale along the way, so I would be more audible. Most deaf people tend to hold their breath while talking because they cannot hear how consonants are supposed to be exhaled. In fact, young deaf children have to be taught to blow, even to blow out their birthday candles. They do know to round their lips but they don't realize when blowing is supposed to occur. The sight of a feather fluttering from being blown can help.

Because many deaf people do not breathe correctly when they speak, they end up having weak diaphragms, which inhibits their ability to project their voices across a distance. I was once sitting in a school bus as it waited at a red light and happened to see my mother walking down the street. Opening the window, I yelled,

"Hey, Mom!" But she didn't hear, even though I was only thirty feet away. A hearing friend sitting next to me watched me try a few more times with my voice raised at the highest volume. She then leaned over and yelled, "Hey Mom!" My mother turned her head, puzzled because she didn't recognize the voice. I sank in my seat, my face bright red!

As I worked with Beth, I also did relaxation exercises with my often restricted voice. I tended to tense my throat during speaking, which Beth suspected had been happening nearly all my life. The habit would be impossible to eliminate during only two weeks of speech therapy, so Beth made me promise to continue relaxation exercises after I had gone back home. Relaxing my throat was still difficult to do all the way through college where I often felt insecure and uptight. Now, I can relax my voice, but only when I'm in a pleasant mood. You don't want to hear how my voice sounds when I want to strangle someone or kick a trash can.

In addition, Beth informed me that I was still omitting some consonant sounds like the NG sound and a final G. Beth also had to teach me what to do with my tongue to produce a perfect CH and J, which wasn't easy. I had trouble making a correct S sound when another consonant followed immediately, for example ST, SK, and other blends; however, Beth had an S indicator, a device the size of a cigarette pack that blinked its red light when I correctly made the sound, which was an enormous help. Somehow, we managed to squeeze in work on all these errors during our therapy, and Beth really did work hard to motivate me. In fact, a speech therapy career might even be more laborious than one hauling sacks of cement mix.

Harvey and Nash had moved back home after graduating from their colleges. The house had been awfully quiet with only me and my parents for a long time, so I was delighted to have my brothers again under the roof. Lindsay was about five miles away in his tiny apartment; however, he came over frequently to catch up with the family. Mom and Dad had been great company during my bad days, but I had long ached for a sibling to share secrets, to tell dirty jokes, and most of all, to laugh with. I just wanted a lively atmosphere to get rid of the blues and needed my brothers for a good laugh.

Even in his mid-twenties, Harvey never tired of beating me up or pulling jokes on me. But fortunately, I had either Nash or Lindsay running to protect me. They would pound on Harvey, rattling the whole house. I'd never forget the clever trick Lindsay did to protect me. One night, Harvey seemed bored around the house, so he decided to prey on me while I was doing homework in my room. Knowing that I could not hear him come in, he sneaked up behind me and said "Boo!" My shriek was loud enough to alert Lindsay who came running in and tossed Harvey out of the room. Lindsay and I then cast worried looks at each other, knowing that Harvey could sneak back in since we all knew I couldn't hear the doorknob turning.

A quick thinker, Lindsay grabbed a ball of string and tied one end to the lamp on my desk and the other to the doorknob. My room looked like some old yard with a clothesline running across. Lindsay hung a folded paper over the string close to my lamp and told me to holler when the paper went down. After he left, I kept my eyes open for the movement. As you would expect, the paper collapsed and I hollered. Harvey stood there shocked, his hand on the doorknob. Then came a loud *Thud!* There was Lindsay, crashing headlong into Harvey, and they slid ten feet across the floor.

With my brothers around, my social life had more good days than bad because I was able to turn to them for advice. I had a good junior year not only because of the social life but also because I had made good grades and it was now time to start thinking about college. I already knew what kind of career

I wanted in the future: landscape design. This type of job, I assumed, would be beneficial for me because it required sight but not necessarily hearing. When I was eleven, a landscape designer drew up a plan for my mother's backyard. I was fascinated with this large blueprint full of lines and shapes. My eyes studied it inch by inch.

My family in 1978. From left to right: Harvey,
Nash, Lindsay, Mom, me, and Dad.

I was all geared up for college hunting, but something worried me sick: my low score on the scholastic aptitude test, which could have quashed my dreams of going to a good college. That SAT had been a four-hour nightmare while I racked my brain and chewed on pencils. I would never take it again, even if someone put a gun to my head. All the other aptitude tests I had taken at Garrison-Williams and Collegiate were a nightmare, too.

That's because these tests contained mostly verbal content. V-e-r-b-a-l: Something that seems impossible for deaf people.

I had gotten extremely low scores on every one of the aptitude tests, which had never surprised me. I took my SAT score with an Oh-well-what-can-I-do? attitude, but even so, my low score shocked me. I didn't even make it to 800, half of the maximum score. Anyone who scored 1600 on an SAT must have had very good ears!

Mom and Dad told me not to dwell so much on the SAT score and be optimistic because of my school grades, so we took off for a weekend of college-hunting as soon as I started my senior year. We had been told that Virginia Tech had disability services and could possibly help me out with expenses. And more important, this school had one of the top five horticultural education programs in the country.

After visiting a few other universities that seemed reluctant to accept a deaf person, I was deeply worried when we arrived at Virginia Tech, and I prayed that this place would accept me. We were given directions to the Equal Opportunity-Affirmative Action office on the edge of the huge campus. A brunette lady greeted us at the front desk and introduced herself as an assistant for the Handicap Concerns Officer who was not in at that time. Every time I think about her these days, my mind replays the powerful scene in which she really buoyed my hopes for the future.

After apologizing for her boss's absence, the lady offered to look at my grade report. She took one look and raised her hands in absolution and said, "You will be accepted." My heart suddenly leaped. She repeated this sentence in an adamant way, even though I had not applied to this university yet. She also assured me that there was no need to worry about my SAT score and that I would receive plenty of help here through note takers and private tutors, all paid by the university. The lady had said it so forthrightly that I had to believe it. And she was right!

A DIFFERENT WORLD

Before even setting foot in college, I was preoccupied with the exciting future of independence awaiting me. But when I arrived on Virginia Tech campus with all my luggage, my excitement turned to fear. Strangers were everywhere, strangers who obviously did not have any experience with a deaf person. I wasn't prepared for this part—being away from home, the place where everyone understood my deafness. I wanted to cling to Mom and Nash who were helping loading things into my dorm room. Relieved to have my oldest brother during our brief campus walk, I listened to Nash's warning that college life could be reckless with tons of alcohol and one-night stands.

When Mom and Nash turned to leave, I felt an instant pang of homesickness, a wrench in my stomach, so sharp that I nearly keeled over. And the lump in my throat was so big that I couldn't swallow. I sure as hell didn't want Mom and Nash to leave; I even considered grabbing my luggage and fleeing back home from my new room. But then I quickly reminded myself that I was an adult, old enough to cope with this rite of passage on my own. My body tensed, trying to resist from running after my family, and I reluctantly waved good-bye to them. It was the worst homesick feeling I had ever had. Being left at Clarke School at the age of five might have been worse, but I don't remember that at all. That departure at Virginia Tech, yes, my memory is so strong that I can still feel my stomach rip.

Wayne Speer, the Handicap Concerns Officer, offered to find me a tutor for every one of my classes, but I declined, assuming that lecture notes and textbooks would help me pull through.

But it helped to have a fellow classmate hand me the notes after each class so I could take them to Wayne's building for free copies. Wayne and I would then discuss my progress in each class. Acting like a concerned parent, he wrote up a list of my classes on the blackboard and asked about the updates. After listening to my reports, he'd tell me that I needed to study harder. Although he didn't have much experience with deafness, I always felt confident with Wayne and considered him a great friend. Before I left his office each time, we swapped tales and shared interests like outdoor adventures.

Despite help from the note takers, college was difficult because it demanded so many things in a short time. I never thought I'd have to read at least five chapters for each test; therefore, my reading pace had to increase for me to keep up. The demands gave me little time to reread and understand the meaning of a sentence or an entire paragraph. And college required so many papers to write. I'd have to turn in a paper almost every week, especially in that loathsome English composition class. My writing skills were still far below average, which was something I tried to hide from others on campus. I had no family to turn to for help and was too embarrassed to ask my dormmates for fear I'd be considered not so smart. They had no idea that deafness caused such difficulty in language development. So I struggled to write papers on my own, cautious not to plagiarize. Sometimes it took me a whole night to finish the first paragraph, and I'd become so frustrated that I'd throw a pencil across the room—only when I was alone— creating a line on the wall.

I was nervous about sharing a room with someone totally unfamiliar with deafness, which I had never done before. I knew that, to the majority, deafness was one of the most intolerable of all disabilities. But my roommate didn't appear to be bothered by my deafness. She was always out working or marching in the school band, which suited me fine.

Always looking for fun and companionship, I turned to the girls in my hall and tried to be like a regular girl. We ate meals at the cafeteria, walked to class together, and checked out bars during happy hour. I usually had a great time with these girls but, still, often felt lonely on the inside. More of a wallflower than a participant, I normally kept quiet around the group. I told myself that I was used to standing back anyway.

As I had expected, none of the girls tried to become real close with me, although they treated me with great kindness. I wasn't angry with them because they didn't grow up with me and were unaware of so many aspects of deafness. That's why my college friends were different from those back at home. It was no surprise to me that the invisible wall I had built around myself got thicker. It would take me years to push it down, making myself more available emotionally and not worrying about what kind of friend I was. Today, however, the college friends with whom I've kept in touch are no different than my hometown friends.

Social life was even harder because Blacksburg was all parties, at somebody's apartment or at a fraternity house. With the rock music blaring at 115 decibels, I couldn't communicate, and my unmonitored voice was often drowned out. I usually clammed up and entertained my talk-devoid mind by staring at people and studying their body language. It was an interesting diversion; however, I tried not to stare too long. I knew it would irritate people and it'd be an invasion of privacy. But hey, it was fun to watch how people conversed with physical language. Looking sideways with a lowered gaze, I could tell when a couple was arguing; their heaving chests and tightened lips revealed the clues.

The ear-splitting parties were not always fun, but I figured it'd be better to hang out with friends than stay alone in my room. I started drinking a lot, way too much at a time. I drank more than I talked. I took too many sips without pausing to say something. It wouldn't be worth trying to converse in a loud atmosphere. It did make me angry not being able to communicate, so I thought five or six beers would lessen my frustration or even totally wipe it out. Then the next morning I'd wake up in my own bed (if luck would have it) and wonder why the ceiling lamp moved like an amoeba. When I'd sit up, a massive hangover would hit me, shooting a jab of pain through the side of my head. Gosh, I hated that feeling. But it happened again and again. As a matter of fact, I turned to alcohol to avoid not only the communication hassles but also the blues that were becoming more and more frequent.

I joined a sorority called Delta Delta Delta, looking forward to interacting with a variety of girls. Fortunately, my hometown friend Mary Park was in my pledge class, and it was a relief to have someone who understood deafness. Mary had been one of my best friends since I came home from Clarke, and we attended the same schools, playing basketball together. She would eventually become my roommate for eight years after college until I tied the knot with Steve.

During my pledge period I grew comfortable with the sisters, especially when speaking on a one-on-one basis. But still, I remained painfully shy in a group. While introducing ourselves at the first meeting, I was scared to death of speaking in front of these girls. My whole body trembled inside, nerves jabbing each other like lightning bolts. I was so self-conscious of my deaf voice, I even thought about escaping the room. When it was my turn to speak, I inhaled to calm my frazzled nerves and talked so fast that it went like a blur. I just wanted to get it over with, and I didn't worry whether or not the girls understood me. I didn't have the guts to look the girls in the eye when speaking.

Then I met my big sister Faith Rios and immediately liked her elaborate way of teaching me about the sorority—its bylaws, purposes, symbols, and all that. Faith was, and is, one of the easiest people to lipread; she's got incredibly readable lips that would break into a cute smile. As my pledge period proceeded, Faith came by my room with sentimental cards and presents before lecturing on whatever I was supposed to learn.

I received a letter from Cheryl saying she had also joined a sorority at National Technical Institute for the Deaf in New York. NTID is a part of Rochester Institute of Technology, where deaf students often participate in classes with hearing students. It took me by surprise because Cheryl was in a deaf college after spending a decade in regular school. I fearfully wondered if she had returned to the deaf world, but let it go because Cheryl sounded happy in her letters, especially compared to her high school days when she expressed her frustration in writing.

For the past few years I had not heard much from Diane and wondered how she was handling the hearing world. She responded to my letters but never really elaborated on this issue. Switching from deaf school to regular school at the age of sixteen was certainly not a breeze. Not wanting to pester, I continued writing to Diane—and to Cheryl— just to say hello and tell them about my struggle in the hearing world. We had always written to each other when we felt the blues, sharing hearing-world experiences. I wanted to tell my deaf friends what I had here was definitely no piece of cake.

Because pledging took so much time, my grades started slipping and I was down in the dumps. This period was one of the hardest times of my life. I can't blame it on the sorority; it was my whole self. I was lacking motivation, and there was no family to kick my butt. Here in college I had no discipline and didn't study as much as I should have. I was skipping many classes, although I knew it was a dumb thing to do. Still, I believed it would be a waste of time to go to class and not understand anything. So I stayed in my room reading magazines or walking downtown; my mind just drifted lazily, not worrying about what I was missing.

I made a mistake by putting social life ahead of school. It had been the top priority from day one. I knew it was wrong, but I had this disability that required a battle for acceptance. I desperately wanted to fit in. I had some close friends, both at home and in college, and I knew they cared about me. And, I cared about them, too. But here, I considered myself a loner, feeling different from everyone around me. I felt completely insecure, and I constantly worried about what people thought of me. Yet, I tried hard to fit in—sometimes too hard.

Not wanting any sympathy, I hid my moodiness and put on a smiling face. Sometimes I felt good about myself when passing a test or having dinner with a friend. But other times, more often than not, I had no self-esteem. Most of all, my deafness made me feel like a ten-year-old around hearing people because I usually got upset over stupid little things and made a big deal out of something that no one else would really pay attention to. I was emotionally immature. Perhaps if I had heard how people reacted to things in a mature way, I wouldn't have dwelled so much on things not worth worrying about.

Even when in a good mood, I still felt immature. I know I had made some people mad without meaning to, or I must have hurt their feelings when I really didn't mean to. Once I made some remarks to a friend, which I thought was just playful verbal teasing; my heart sank when she gave an offended look. Even as a twenty-one-year-old, I had not yet learned those verbal rights and wrongs.

Constant worrying about social life, I continued to do poorly in school and drink heavily at parties. Alone in my room, I'd break down in tears, cursing my own disability. When friends noticed my anguish, I'd just tell them it was because of my academic difficulties. I avoided mentioning my insecurity as a deaf person. Obviously, some of my friends worried about me and my drinking yet seemed afraid to say anything.

One night, I received a call from Faith who expressed her concern about my grades. As my big sister warned, I would not be initiated in the sorority if I didn't make good grades. Her call scared me into wanting to change my studying habits. At about the same time, Wayne beckoned me to his office and asked why I was having a hard time. I wept and confessed cutting classes, explaining the reason for it. He gently pressed that I still needed to go to class even if I didn't understand because not going at all would take away more motivation. A few professors had called him, expressing concern about my frequent absences, so that meant they cared, Wayne told me.

Wayne once again suggested that I get a tutor for every class. He explained that most professors hardly paid attention to text-books, depending on their own lectures. And the students didn't always jot down everything, so that's why I had missed quite a bit. To my realization, college was mostly verbal, different from high school where textbooks were usually dependable. However, Wayne advised reading textbooks for the sake of information. As I listened, I thought about my parents who had sent me a heart-felt letter of encouragement. Just then, I felt a jolt of motivation, realizing everyone wanted me to do well here at Virginia Tech. There would be support all the way to graduation. I finally agreed on tutors and promised Wayne to do better, taking the last tissue from his Kleenex™ box.

My grades had improved after I started working with Martha, a fellow horticulture major, who deliberately explained the notes with enthusiasm. She was an excellent tutor and also a great friend. We decided to take elective classes together, one of which was, well, a very popular one: Human Sexual Development. Martha didn't have to tutor a whole lot on that one because most of the material came from the textbook and of course, "X-rated" videos.

To my mother's horror, I was taking another sinful course at the same time: Wines and Vines. Yes, Martha had to teach me all the complicated wine-making stuff while we were in a lab mashing grapes. When I came home, Dad said I had better learn a lot about wine and sex because he had paid for it. I hadn't told my parents about registering for those courses until they started.

Whenever I showed Wayne my test grades, he crossed his arms and gave me that big I-told-you-so grin. Okay, I learned a lesson, I admitted, and asked him to get me more tutors. School was moving right along, and I had made the grade to join the TriDelta sisterhood. With better grades and a sorority membership, I was beginning to feel more settled at Virginia Tech, although I still occasionally felt blue when my social life would take a turn downward. But now, the number one priority was school, not how I could fit in.

People asked me "What is your major?" over-emphasizing the last word with questioning faces. To me, it seemed as though they were asking what I, a deaf person, was doing here in college. One half of me felt offended and the other half felt proud. The proud half could prove that I was just like them, able to strive for a college degree. Imagine what they would say if I replied, "Physics."

If I hadn't joined the sorority, I don't know what my life would be like at this moment. TriDelta really changed my life in many positive ways, giving me a chance to cope better with deafness. I had an opportunity to learn to deal with all kinds of personalities—and to read lips of all shapes and movements. With my good hearing aids, I learned to understand who was speaking, especially at meetings, by the different tones of each person's voice; I could hear the voice better than words. In fact, watching others speak prepared me for the future in the working world.

It took me a while to have the guts to speak in front of a large audience. I remember the first time I did it. Normally, my sisters and I formed a large circle at the end of a meeting to announce or say whatever we wanted. If we wanted to say something, we would hold the gavel until we were finished and then pass it on.

For a long time, I had been mute and had treated the gavel like burning firewood, passing it along as fast as I could. But that night, I wanted to tell my sisters about the strange dream I had about a sorority event. I held the gavel, ready to speak, and that just about shocked everybody's pants off. They stared at me in disbelief, mouths half-open. I told about my dream, feeling nervous and trying not to talk too fast. To my enormous relief, everyone laughed and hooted. After that, I no longer stood there like a standup board figure.

When it was time for me to take on the responsibility for a little sister, I wondered with concern how I could handle the advising as a deaf person. I was relieved when I was paired with a little sister named Kathy Hyland because she was sweet and patient. I tried to teach her the same way Faith taught me. It was completely weird to teach someone because, all my life, I had been the one who was taught. For the first time, I had responsibilities for another human being; that gave me a shot of self-esteem. I wanted to be worthy and dependable to someone, and I loved it!

My sorority occasionally gave low-key parties in the daytime, and these helped me to learn to monitor my voice and talk with less difficulty. The sun's rays shining through the room also made it easier to lipread, but I could never understand people with the window or lamp behind them. They looked like silhouettes in front of the glare, making lipreading impossible. Most often, I'd have to ask people to step away from the window or lamp, but sometimes, I'd sneak around to have my back to the light.

Lipreading is definitely more laborious than hearing. Some people are hard to lipread. I have to watch the movements of lips, teeth, tongue, and cheeks, and decipher every word that is spoken. It wears me out, and before too long, I can feel my brain turning into mush. That's why I envy hearing people who are able to understand words without relying on their eyes. Some hearing friends tell me that listening can be difficult, too. I'm sure it is—at times. But for me, every day is filled with trying to lipread all the look-alike sounds and maneuvering to see everything that is spoken—trivial or not—while piecing together information and trying to keep up with a communication flow that continuously races ahead. And that constant challenge can take its toll.

At first, I was frustrated for not being able to understand what people said and went home to discuss it with Mom. She advised that I just smile and nod, even if words zoomed over my head. So then I went back to school and grinned, bobbing my head like a jack-in-the-box. Finally, a friend had the heart to tell me not to do that. She warned, what if a guy asked you to sleep with him and you grinned, your head bouncing? I gasped in horror and went home to tell Mom that her advice was the worst advice she had ever given. As I later realized, hearing people also just smile and nod to deaf people because they are afraid to hurt feelings if they ask for a repetition. (Often, deaf people sense that and repeat anyway.) So both deaf and hearing people can sometimes look like fools.

I learned from sorority parties that I could get away with not understanding someone without having to grin and nod. I learned how to handle a blabbermouth by looking interested while words flew over my head. Whenever that person paused, I'd raise my eyebrows and say, "Oh really?" or tilt my head back with a low "Eh-heh." I still do that; it helps me look polite, not bored or plain worn out.

During my sorority days, I learned to love round tables. You guessed it, a round table gives me a chance to see everybody's lips. A small square table is okay, much better than a rectangular one. I avoid sitting in the middle of a long rectangular table because my neck and muscles become stiff from switching back and forth like a water sprinkler. Instead, I try to take a seat next to or at the head of the table where I can keep my neck at a comfortable angle and move only my eyes around.

As a Handicap Concerns Officer, Wayne's primary goal was to make students and faculty more aware of the disabled population on campus, so he decided to sponsor Virginia Tech's first "Handicap Awareness Day." During my four years at Tech, I watched Wayne struggle to make the campus more disabled-friendly by building wheelchair ramps and curb cuts. His work was driven by subsection 504 of the Rehabilitation Act of 1973, which forbade discrimination against disabled individuals in any program using federal money.

On "Handicap Awareness Day," I attended a luncheon where there was a panel discussion on accessibility problems in Blacksburg; then later, I watched a wheelchair basketball game in which a men's wheelchair basketball team played against Tech's regular women's team. Much to my surprise, several of my sorority sisters showed up at the game because of me. I didn't tell them anything about this special event; they just came. I was deeply moved and appreciated my sisters for coming to support.

But it was a depressing day for me because everyone was looking at me as a handicapped person. To tell the truth, the terms *handicapped* or *disabled* always haunted me. Although I did have a disability, I just couldn't imagine myself in the same category as those in wheelchairs. I badly wanted to be considered a regular girl, that's all. That's why I was tearfully bummed out that night, lying to concerned friends that I was upset because of a poor test grade. (Wayne, it wasn't your fault for holding a handicapped awareness day. It was me, just young and emotionally immature. I would've felt proud today, since I have grown to accept my disability. You did a great job.)

I never told anyone about my real feelings as a deaf person, not even my mother, not even when I broke down in front of someone every once in a while. I expressed only my frustration, but never how I fully felt as a deaf person. Nobody suspected any conflict because I was normally a happy-looking person and readily admitted my deafness, even joking about it. But the truth is, I was often ashamed of my disability.

I was embarrassed enough to avoid the other two deaf students on campus, trying to blend in with the majority. One was a really shy girl, and the other was a handsome bodybuilder; they both could talk and lipread. I wonder how the girl felt about being one of the three deaf students at this large university; she was so shy and reserved that I couldn't guess. But the bodybuilder, I could see how he felt—exactly the same way I did; he tried to avoid me, too. The bodybuilder and I somehow knew the same people and occasionally ended up at the same parties. Whenever he saw me, he'd quickly avert his eyes and walk away into his crowd. That didn't offend me because I understood. We were both trying to blend with the hearing people.

No one knew, but I was often angry about having this disability and struggled to keep it to myself. I'd sometimes explode alone in my room, throwing things and smacking my fist into my hand and whispering a string of obscenities—all in silence because I didn't want anyone to know. When I watched people conversing with such ease at a loud party, I'd get so livid that I thought about finding a baseball bat or a heavy tree branch and smashing the blaring speakers into smithereens. I even came close to it a few times.

I envied hearing people for their easy abilities to communicate with one another. I admit it was intense envy. It bothered me to watch people carry on conversation a hundred feet apart or from different rooms, without having to look at each other. And these people didn't have to struggle to be patient as I always did—most of the time without luck. Unhappy about having this much-ignored disability, I often wondered what it would be like to be hearing—so nice and easy.

Honest to say, I sometimes felt a spark of anger toward God, but that never lasted more than a few seconds. I tried hard not to blame Him for my disadvantages and this difficult disability. I tried to remind myself of good things He had done for me: giving me a loving, supportive family, especially my wonderful mother, who couldn't prevent the disability from occurring during her pregnancy. I was extremely grateful for my good functional family and loved them with all my heart.

But my family didn't know what it was like being deaf. That's why I sometimes felt isolated from them. I never told them of my feelings. Years later, my parents and I talked about how I had "successfully" pulled through as a deaf person. When I finally told them it wasn't all that rosy in the past, Mom disagreed, saying I was just fine with hardly a sign of distress. So I showed her a part of my unpublished novel, based on deafness, in which all the deep feelings spilled out. After reading it, Mom looked at me in surprise and remarked, "I didn't know you were depressed."

Not everyone in my family was always patient with me, and I wasn't always patient with them either. We have had screaming fights, not speaking to each other for days. However, there is an incredibly powerful bond between us; we just forgive and forget. We try to help each other get over hard times and look to the future. If I had told my family about my feelings as a deaf person, they would have offered emotional support but also would have firmly persuaded me to quit moping around and try to make the best of it.

After four years of muddling through parties and books, I managed to earn a bachelor's degree in landscape horticulture. During my last year, I had a variety of tutors for my horticulture classes. I less frequently came bursting into Wayne's office in tears to complain about a test or some hard-nosed professor. With all his caring, Wayne had made the college graduation possible, and I was grateful enough to give him and his wife a farewell gift.

With a college degree, I vowed to change myself as a person and cut down on my drinking, learning when to stop. I'd had enough of watching the ceiling lamp move like an amoeba every weekend morning. Now that I was back in my hometown where everyone was understanding of my handicap, I determined to stop worrying so much about fitting in and try to maintain a high level of self-esteem. Most of all, I wanted to be more emotionally stable, and if anything went wrong, I'd go to my family.

THREE PATHS

Once settled at home, I decided to take a vacation before my job search. My idea was to drive up to Massachusetts and visit Cheryl and Diane whom I hadn't seen for six years. Although that time was the longest we had been separated, we had managed to keep in touch by mail. But letters hadn't been enough. I had to see them.

Solitude was something I had long grown accustomed to, even with great pleasure; therefore, I wouldn't mind driving by myself. Equipped with the AAA maps, I convinced my worried parents that I would handle the road trip by staying with several friends along the way. After contacting these friends by phone, I had my two-week vacation mapped out day by day.

First I stopped in Philadelphia to see Faith who had moved there for her job. Another sorority girl Susan joined us for a weekend visit. That wasn't the first time the three of us had visited together far from our hometowns. We had once traveled in Spain where I had to grapple with a foreign language, but Faith and Susan, with their good ability to speak Spanish, had alleviated the situation by teaching me one sentence: No hablo Español. Sure enough, that sentence, (which translated, "I don't know Spanish"), quieted the fast-talking natives every time I said it. Although I had been to Philadelphia a hundred times before, I had never gotten beyond the airport where I had changed flights between Clarke School and home. So in a sense, I once more visited a new place with them and was delighted to see the Liberty Bell for the first time.

Next I drove up to Massachusetts, cutting through New York City and listening to the Rolling Stones at full blast. I stopped in Boston to visit my high school friend Elizabeth who had decided to settle there after college. Still fancy-free and footloose, we spent a few days shopping and barhopping. From Boston, I drove west to Greenfield to reunite with Cheryl and her family. When I pulled into their driveway, I felt like a long-departed seaman coming home. Mr. Robbins stood there with his eyes watering; it really choked me up to see a grown man that way. Then I met Cheryl's fiancé Rick and couldn't get over the fact that one of my earliest best friends was getting married. Rick was also deaf and hailed from Ohio. He had attended NTID with Cheryl and her brother Chuck.

We spent days looking at old photo albums in that same yellow house where I still felt pretty much at home. Chuck brought his year-old daughter Sarah, and it was touching to see Mrs. Robbins, a new grandmother, play with her granddaughter on the grass. Mr. Robbins had not changed; he was still always doing something around the house, whether it was chopping firewood at ten degrees below or hacking tall weeds at above one hundred degrees.

Cheryl and Rick followed me to the Karases' place in Springfield where we reunited with hugs and kisses. It was a captivating moment, and again, I felt welcomed home after a long, long time away. Diane, now married, introduced me to her three-year-old son Artie. I was overwhelmed by Diane's progress to motherhood. We were *old*.

After spending an afternoon with us, Cheryl gave me a sentimental good-bye with the I-love-you sign, which choked me up. We would always care deeply for each other. But I also felt sad, and even worried, about our friendship because we were now in totally different worlds. Cheryl had switched to the deaf signing world, using sign language with her college friends. Fortunately, she hadn't given up oralism completely; we could still lipread together. Nevertheless, the last time I had seen her, she had hearing friends; now there were none, it seemed to me. And she was going to marry a deaf guy which would bring her deeper into the deaf world. At that time, I didn't understand the term *Deaf community*. Without my realizing it, however, Cheryl had joined a world with its own language and culture.

I managed to brush off the situation and savored my time with Diane and her family, once again devouring Mrs. Karas' Polish sausage and sharing jokes with Mr. Karas. With Diane's brothers joining us, we spent a day on the lake, waterskiing and barbecuing. I had a chance to talk with Diane's husband Butch whom she had met in high school. I felt comfortable with Butch and liked him as a person.

When Diane and I settled to talk at her apartment, I expressed my bafflement about Cheryl joining the deaf world. Diane assumed that, because Cheryl's brother had gone to NTID, she had decided to follow in his footsteps. Little sister following big brother was what we concluded. After trading our concerns, Diane and I shrugged helplessly and figured we'd have to just let it go. Deep down in my heart, I still felt let down because Cheryl and I had spent years writing letters about hearing-world experiences. But now, we could no longer do that.

Back at home, I told Mom about Cheryl and about my fearing that our long friendship could possibly dwindle. Mom assured me that it would not happen if Cheryl and I kept writing to each other like old times, as if nothing had happened. She made the point that Cheryl may have decided to give up the hearing culture because she was profoundly deaf, not hard of hearing like me and Diane. The hearing world must have been much more difficult for Cheryl, Mom said. Realizing that Cheryl was too important a friend to relinquish, I vowed to keep writing and visiting her. I told Mom how grateful I was for the talk; Mom told me to stop worrying about Cheryl—and find a job.

As I planned for job hunting, I braced myself for introducing myself to strangers on the phone, which I had never done before. Now that I was a college graduate off to independence, I declined my mother's offer to contact landscaping companies for me. I wanted to try it myself and practice expanding my voice to a professional tone without quivering. Over the years, I had always been afraid to talk too loud and, therefore, was a low talker, which caused people to lean over or tell me to speak up.

The other concern, of course, involved my ability to understand what strangers were saying. On the phone, I've had to struggle to hear, not lipread. I can hear on the phone for two reasons: first, it's closer to my ear, and second, there is no sound feedback. Without feedback, I can easily recognize people's voices as well as their laughs most of the time. But still, I have trouble distinguishing vowel and consonant sounds on the phone.

When I started talking on the phone, Mom had an amplifier installed in our kitchen phone. Most of the time I had the amplifier turned all the way up and forgot to turn it off when finished. Then some poor member of the family would pick up the ringing phone and hear the caller's blasting hello in the receiver. To my dismay, I had seen every one of my family, at one time or another, suddenly fling the phone at arm's length and look at me as if they were about to wring my neck.

It's funny how some people relate the term *deaf* or even *hard of hearing* to no hearing at all—nothing, zero, zilch. They don't realize that many deaf people can be helped by amplification and that every deaf person has a different degree of hearing loss. So anyway, I've had people look at me in total shock when I talk on the phone or hear a jumbo jet zooming overhead. They ask me, amazed, how I can hear, and I politely tell them that I'm not stone deaf, pointing to my hearing aid.

My job-hunting phone calls led me to a small landscaping company where, relying on my eyes, I learned to design and plant.

I was pleased that my landscape design career was enabling me to deal with clients on a one-on-one basis. Fortunately, I was able to communicate well with most clients, except some elderly people who often presented special challenges. Once, I had a ninety-five-year-old client who was so hunched over when walking that she talked with her head down. Well, I had to walk that way, too, holding a clipboard to my side, so I would be able to look at her lips. We looked like a pair of question marks moving very slowly through her rose garden.

Two of my long-time friends and I found an apartment in Ghent, a popular section of Norfolk, Virginia. I was delighted to room with Mary Park and Molly Hubard since we had grown up together in the same neighborhood. Back in high school, we drove around doing pranks like flying our brassieres on the antenna. And Mary was the one who had pledged with me in the sorority at Tech. I certainly looked forward to pure entertainment from those two girls after a long day's work.

Our den had a fake furnace, shaped like a funnel extending to the ceiling, and we wondered why the landlord had stuck it there. One hot summer night, Molly and I figured out what to do with the furnace, so we dragged it to Mary's bedroom while she was out. We taped a note on it saying that a cold front was coming and we wanted her to stay warm, signing the note with "Your considerate loving roommates." Imagine how Mary felt when she walked in and saw that monstrous black thing next to her bed!

Another night after Molly had gone out, Mary and I stuffed a pair of jeans and connected boots to them. We placed this partial dummy under Molly's bed so it would look like a dead man with his legs poking out. Mary heard the door open, and we dove into her bedroom next to Molly's. We sat waiting in the pitch dark, trying not to make any sound. I tapped Mary, turning my palms in puzzlement. At first, Mary tried to whisper into my ear, but it was no use. So she flung her hands in the air, making some kind of gesture. Once, again, I tapped Mary, again flipping up my palms. She repeated all her indecipherable gestures over her head. It turned out that Molly had not yet seen the "dead person" because she went straight to the shower. When we emerged from the bedroom, Mary exhaled in exhaustion and declared, "I'm not ever going to talk to you in the dark again."

Now that I had a closed caption decoder, given to me by my parents, it helped that my roommates liked to watch the same TV shows as me. That decoder really changed my life, providing a much broader view of the everyday world. Seeing dialogue word by word greatly improved my language. I could also understand jokes better. Now, I understood the jokes and didn't have to fake a laugh. Long before depending on the close caption, I could understand most of the dialogue in only one type of TV show: Soap operas. My college roommates, Nancy and Reba Ann, and I were huge fans of *Guiding Light* and even rushed home after class to watch it. Well, Nancy and Reba Ann never had to explain to me what was going on in that show because I could perfectly understand just about every single line. Why? Because all the characters in any soap opera always *yell* at each other.

In my new home, I was pretty well equipped with special devices for the hearing impaired. I had a phone amplifier and a digital alarm clock with a small flash, even more powerful than a camera flash. Now that I had this clock, I was thrilled about not having my roommates wake me up. My brother Harvey had found it at the Gallaudet bookstore and gave it to me for Christmas. When he came across this clock, an excited signing clerk explained how it worked by widening her eyes and exploding her hands outward. Yes, it was blindingly bright!

All of my brothers and I lived within only one mile of one another, and my parents had moved to a townhouse within walking distance. We regularly met at Lindsay's raw bar for a few drinks or a birthday party. I felt blessed to have the whole family close together in the same area. Nash and his wife Vickie often had a cookout where we gathered on the deck until sunset, sharing jokes and current events.

One night, Lindsay took me to watch *It's a Wonderful Life*. My brother explained the movie plot (I knew he had rehearsed doing it) while we waited for it to begin. I watched how George Bailey was led by the angel Clarence through a totally different setting. That movie left me profoundly touched and became one of my favorites. If it weren't for Lindsay's consideration, I wouldn't have any idea why Clarence popped out of the blue, much less understand his angel identity or why the town suddenly turned harsh with all the brooding people amid those Christmas decorations.

My social life in the hearing world had improved because I had more emotional security and no longer worried what people thought of me. And I no longer tried to please impatient or mean people. Most of all, I'd learned to be myself instead of trying to blend in. I feel fortunate to have kept, even to this day, both new and old close friends with whom I can dine, mostly on a one-on-one basis. But I always enjoy a trio lunch with my childhood friends Nancy Nusbaum and Helen Roberts, who always have the patience to talk slowly throughout the whole meal. There has never been a lunch without us teasing one another; no wonder Nancy, Helen, and I are usually the rowdiest customers at every quiet restaurant.

As I remember it, almost perfectly, March 1988 was a dramatic month because so many things happened—all having to do with deafness. The first event was thoroughly encouraging for my self-esteem; the second, shocking yet later successful; and the third, extremely discouraging. It's just a crazy coincidence that all these events occurred in a short time but at least it helps me remember them well.

With saved money, I decided to buy a small pickup truck that I could use to carry plants. Dad offered to go with me, but

I wanted to try buying the truck myself. Of course, I was edgy about buying a vehicle on my own, especially deciding how to make installments, signing contracts, and all that—and most important, handling all the communication. But it helped to collect advice from friends beforehand so I was prepared not to have any misunderstanding with car salesmen, some of whom could be pushy for a young single woman like myself.

It took me about a week to narrow my search down to one dealership that offered the best price on a new Chevy truck. In truth, I had trouble understanding everything the salesman said from the start because he talked pretty fast. That's why I was set to review every single bit of the contract and see what options such as AC were included and, of course, what type of monthly payment I would have to make. After reading the contract several times, I felt confident to sign and make a down payment. In a few days I brought home a new truck, equipped with everything I asked for. The whole thing gave me a huge notch of self-esteem because I had handled it without help from anybody. As a deaf person, I felt buoyant for signing a big contract for the first time, instead of depending on others.

Then Gallaudet University became the focus of the world. Watching the news, I was amazed by the marching deaf students with big banners emblazoned with DEAF PRESIDENT NOW! At first, I wondered how would a deaf college president be able to handle such a huge responsibility? Communication would be the main issue. I thought these marching students were unrealistic until I learned that Gallaudet had hired a woman president who had no experience with deaf people. A president who knew absolutely *nothing* about deafness, much less how to communicate? I could not believe it. Despite her good resume, she did not belong at Gallaudet. As I watched the news of her unwelcome entry to Gallaudet, I felt sorry for her, but I could feel my heart marching with the students.

Caught up in the headlines, I realized that Gallaudet consisted of a deaf community with its own culture and language. The student body and some faculty members had been waiting for a deaf president for years. Under enormous pressure, the mostly hearing board of directors finally dismissed the new president, turning the job over to Irving King Jordan, Jr., a deaf man who had worked there as dean of the college of arts and sciences. I began to believe that he would work out because Dr. Jordan knew what it was like having this disability and would be able to respond to the students' needs. Those marching students certainly got what they wanted, and this showed the true confidence of the deaf community.

As soon as the Gallaudet hype lessened, my grandmother began to have difficulty breathing and was rushed to the emergency room. While waiting in the lobby, I was approached by a nurse who informed me that the doctors had told her of my hearing impairment. She explained that there was a deaf AIDS patient in the other room who was trying to tell them about the medicine he had been taking, but no one could understand him. The nurse asked if I knew sign language. Feeling uncertain, I admitted knowing only fingerspelling, which wouldn't help much because of its slow pace and complicated method. Then with a flicker of hope, I suggested a notepad but was crushed when the nurse replied she already tried that, only to find that this AIDS patient was illiterate.

After regretfully explaining to the nurse that I wouldn't be of any use, I plopped down in the chair and buried my head in my hands. I had never felt so guilty before and was mad at myself for not knowing sign language. But moments later, my feeling of guilt was replaced by shock and anger. Why didn't the hospital have an interpreter? I looked around, disgusted. The hospital should've thought of identifying one or two staff members to learn sign language so an interpreter would be available at all times. I was pretty sure that some of those hospital staff had learned to speak French or Spanish for the sake of communicating with foreign patients. It wouldn't hurt to learn sign language, although it may require daily practice for fluency, even if the person didn't become a certified interpreter.

I still feel contrite whenever I think about that deaf AIDS patient and wonder what became of him. Although I never saw him, I often picture him as a desperate, gaunt man with curly black hair. The thought of the hospital staff, desperate because of the communication problem, giving him the wrong medication or even none at all makes me tremble. I want to say my prayers are with him, although I don't know his fate. Today, that emergency-room scene would have turned out differently because I now know sign language.

Mary and I continued living together after Molly got married and moved away. So another friend Barbara moved in with us. Soon, we all had to move out because the new landlord wanted to convert our place into a condo, so we settled in our second apartment just across the street. A while later, Barbara married and moved out. Mary and I couldn't find another roommate, so we moved a mile away to our third apartment for better rent. I had all of my brothers move the furniture every time we relocated, providing pizza to keep them happy, although they still cussed like sailors as they hauled our massive sofa up stairs and through narrow doorways.

A few months into our third apartment, Mary heard something right above her bedroom. It was the couple who lived above us enjoying their bed, if you know what I mean. When Mary first described the noises to me, we fell to the floor in laughter. But then the sounds became too frequent, much to Mary's irritation. When we were sitting in the den, she'd suddenly drop a magazine on her lap and growl, "Here they go again." I felt bad for her having to listen to all this and even apologized for my deafness.

Glaring at me in envy, Mary had me stand in her bedroom and told me to turn my hearing aid all the way up. Sure enough, I heard it, loud and clear, but only if I stood in that spot. Considering my hearing roommate's lack of sleep, I offered to trade my bedroom, but Mary assumed that the honeymoon would soon be over. And she was right. The noises eventually turned to loud bickering and then silence. It was good to see Mary smile again in the mornings.

Mary occasionally went away for several days, and I had to adjust to being alone in the apartment. I wasn't too concerned about safety. But the problem was, I yearned to hear something in this lonely place. I had been taught to hear things with pleasure. So I'd talk to my cat Ernie, just to hear my own voice. I'd say to him, "So! How was your day? Slept and ate all day? Look at you, you've got a wonderful life sitting on your butt and not having to work." If Ernie could understand what I was telling him, he'd agree and never change that kind of life.

I know I could have turned on the stereo just to hear something, but I was always afraid to miss an expected phone call or a warning sound such as the disposal being accidentally left on—which I had done before. The disposal in this apartment ran with such little sound that I didn't know it was on. I had brought my landlord in to check the stalled disposal, too embarrassed to give the reason for it. To my relief, he found a lever under the disposal and clicked it back on.

These days, I walk out the door and then pause, unsure if I've left the water running. So I check every sink on all floors because I've always had an enormous fear of turning my place into a raging flood. Even with powerful amplification, I can never hear the low sound of water running. So I check every single faucet, sometimes two or three times—and not by just looking at it. I place my hand under the faucet. I just don't trust my eyes when it comes to clear water, which seems invisible to me.

Cheryl's father died unexpectedly of a heart attack, and the family was quite devastated. Mom contacted Mrs. Robbins by phone to offer our condolences and to invite her and Cheryl to come down for a mother-daughter getaway at our beach cottage in Sandbridge. A few months after the death, Cheryl and her mother flew down and spent a few days alone watching the sunrise and listening to waves as they tried to recover from shock and devastation. My parents and I drove over to treat them to a seafood restaurant where we talked openly about Mr. Robbins's death.

During that visit, I had a better chance to talk with Cheryl, and for the first time, I came to accept her decision to join the deaf community. While we walked on the beach, Cheryl described all the activities with her deaf friends, expressing satisfaction with her social life because she had joined a circle of those with the same disability. It had been four years since she married her deaf husband Rick; Cheryl appeared to be happy with this union. So why should I be upset with Cheryl's decision to join the deaf community if that was what made her happy? By the end of her and her mother's visit to Sandbridge, I felt ecstatic that Cheryl and I could still remain great friends and that I no longer felt awkward about her choice of lifestyle. I finally respected it.

A few months later, I flew to Massachusetts for a respite after going through a horrible breakup with a hearing boyfriend that devastated me to the point where I thought I would never date again. I hadn't often been asked out before I had met this guy; therefore, I was thrilled to date somebody seriously for the first time in a long time. But then, after a year, it wasn't working, and I severed the relationship.

At first, I visited my high school friend Elizabeth who had become Mrs. David Wadman the previous fall. She cheered me up by taking me around Boston for a few days and chatting endlessly about our old days. And then I pitched my tent with Cheryl and Rick, sharing a meaningful conversation through lipreading and some hand gestures. I grew to respect Rick as the guy one of my best friends chose to marry. When we talked about my bad breakup, Rick asked a question that has stuck in my mind for years: "Is it because of deafness?"

That was a good question because most hearing-deaf relationships don't work. They just don't. As shocking as it may sound, hearing-blind relationships work better. You don't need to talk slowly or sign to a blind person, so communication is pretty normal. But with a deaf person, you need patience and tolerance—which didn't exist in my relationship with that guy. He just complained and complained, saying that the problem was much harder for him. Now I look back derisively and say, "Oh, please," while I play an invisible fiddle.

After my stay with Cheryl and Rick, Diane brought me to her house, having invited a few of our Clarke friends for the evening. Before they came, Diane sat me down and said she didn't want me to feel isolated like I did when we were sixteen. Knowing that I was more absorbed in the hearing world than she was, Diane gently explained that she had decided to go "both ways," meaning that she belonged to the hearing world yet had mostly deaf friends she could sign with. If that's what makes her happy, I thought to myself, it's great, go for it. I thanked Diane for the talk and vowed to have a good time no matter what.

That night turned out to be one of the best times I'd ever had in my life. Communication was no problem, really, because I could lipread these friends and vice versa. Despite my lack of signing skills, it was certainly good to be with my deaf friends again. Throughout the evening, Diane kept asking me if I felt out of place to which I answered absolutely not.

I flew home feeling refreshed; visiting old friends certainly was therapeutic. Cheryl was now in the deaf community, and Diane was in between, and I was totally in the hearing world; but they could still remain great friends of mine. No more feelings of isolation or awkwardness. The path we had all started on had eventually separated, slowly but surely, into three paths as we began leading different lives. But our paths would still entwine, and we would always support each other.

A get-together with old friends.
From left to right: Me, Cheryl, and Diane .

THE REUNION

The next drama wouldn't have ensued if Mom had not returned a box of Clarke memorabilia to me. For a couple nights I dug into the cardboard box at my apartment and spread each item on the floor, amazed at how all the items—Miss Miller's weekly letters, my dad's drawings, and all the Polaroids—had stayed in excellent condition, after nearly three decades.

At Mom's suggestion, I wrote an update letter to Clarke, and they responded with the announcement of an upcoming reunion. So I asked Diane and Cheryl by mail if they were coming to this special event. Yes, they were. That prompted my plan to drive up north alone, to visit friends along the way, explore famous gardens to expand my horticultural knowledge, and at last, attend the reunion. So off I went in my little pickup truck at dawn, the rock'n'roll music blaring for the next 700 miles.

I first visited the National Arboretum in Washington, D.C., admiring ancient bonsai and taking notes. My next stop was definitely memorable. It was Gallaudet University, the place I had desperately wanted to visit since the Deaf President Now movement. I parked in front of Chapel Hall, feeling odd, as if I were about to enter a deaf world unlike the one at Clarke. Expecting to see flying hands all around, I braced myself as the lone oralist on this campus. It was such a weird sensation when I entered the open area where summer-school students sat signing on the manicured lawn—all silence. I felt like I'd been dropped from outer space. Even though we all had the same disability, I didn't feel a sense of belonging here. But still, it fascinated me. Why not explore a world I knew absolutely nothing about?

Walking into the bookstore, I noticed the jewelry counter where items depicting the I love you and friend hand signs dominated the display. Each gold earring had the thumb, index finger, and pinky extended, showing a manual alphabet combination of i, l, and y—the I love you sign. Other jewelry had the friend sign in which right and left index fingers interlocked, a perfect sign for closeness.

In the book section, while flipping through a book drawn in sign language, I heard loud grunts and looked over to the next aisle where a couple argued, their hands darting in and out at high speed. I watched sideways with my head down, amazed by the sight of such ferocious signing. And something else struck me: the grunting and hissing sounds the couple made as if they were lifting fifty-pound crates. Why the couple dared to make these grotesque sounds in public was something most hearing people would not understand. I understood. It was because this profoundly deaf couple could not hear themselves and did not know it.

I settled in with coffee at a slow-paced cafeteria and watched a group of students signing across the room. With a small smile, I thought about my past at Clarke where we waved our hands and tapped on shoulders. That's how these Gallaudet students were trying to catch attention, the same way my friends and I did years ago. But here, their signing looked official, unlike the homemade signs at Clarke.

Once in the library, I noticed the door signs saying Classroom on the first floor. Eager to see a deaf college classroom, I sneaked behind a book shelf and watched a small class through an open door. Yes, there was a semicircular pattern of desks, just like at Clarke. But there was no headphone, just hands flying in the air. And the whole atmosphere was dead quiet, not a single voice present. That silence still seemed eerie to me.

The exhibit at the Edward Miner Gallaudet Memorial Building was the most interesting of all. After first admiring historic pictures depicting deaf athletics and early sign language in the hall, I then walked into a room that looked like a hands-on museum. Because this exhibit looked new, I assumed it was set up after the Deaf President Now movement four years earlier.

The next twenty minutes would teach me more about deafness than I had learned in my lifetime. Just standing in this exhibit made me realize there was a *real* deaf culture, something I had never taken seriously before. To my total surprise, I had known very little about my own disability.

I pressed a button on the wall TV and watched thousands of people walking on a New York City sidewalk. The closed caption lines began rolling, "All these people look the same. Do you see any deaf person? You can never tell. Deafness is a hidden handicap." The video continued, explaining that much of the world did not know the complexity of this disability and had trouble understanding it. Absolutely true, I thought with a nod.

Then I turned to the other wall, which bore a large caption: MISCONCEPTIONS ABOUT DEAFNESS. The myths listed below it read:

Deaf people can only do certain jobs.

Deaf people are less intelligent than hearing people.

Deaf people have similar abilities, ideas, and outlooks.

All deaf people use sign language.

All hearing losses are the same.

All deaf people read lips.

Noisy environments don't bother deaf people.

Deaf people can't talk.

Hearing aids restore hearing.

Impressed by this list, I wished I could grab every single soul on earth and bring them in to look at these short yet meaningful misconceptions. This myth wall could totally change the world's perception of deafness in sixty seconds.

Several biographical posters on the other wall caught my eye, since they showed Gallaudet graduates who had achieved high success in the working world. I was awestruck by one poster showing a female lawyer and another showing a male stockbroker and many more. Indeed, deaf people can climb to success just like hearing people.

Later, I met my brother Lindsay at a Baltimore hotel as planned, since he had gone there to attend a Grateful Dead concert the following night, just as he had a million times. His dear wife Koggie, who was no fan of this long-lasting band, had put up with Lindsay's globetrotting but always busied herself with social activities at home to avoid having to go with him. Lindsay had even missed a family picnic for the sake of listening to Jerry Garcia. We had gotten tickets to the Orioles game that night, so Lindsay and I met with his friends for a ride to the game. In the car, I recounted my Gallaudet tour, and one of these friends said he had seen some deaf kids, possibly Gallaudet students, at a Grateful Dead concert, dancing behind the stage with some special vibrating device in their hands.

Years later, I was touched by the movie *Mr. Holland's Opus* in which there was a profoundly deaf boy named Cole. The scene of Cole sitting atop a stereo speaker and shoulder-dancing proved that deaf people, even those who cannot be helped by amplification, *do* love music. Feeling the rhythm of vibrations motivates you to waltz away. Like I've said before, I love music despite incomprehensible lyrics; the instrumental sounds are what attract me. I wonder what it would be like to hold that special device in my hands at a concert. I've learned that hugging a big, sturdy balloon is another way to feel vibrations.

After my visit with Lindsay, I headed northward, and midway, I had to face the anxiety of driving through the Bronx to reach the New York Botanical Gardens. You can't be distracted for a single millisecond on a New York City street because so many cars are swerving in front of you. And the persistent honking! If I ever had to live in this world's noisiest city, my hearing aids would end up in a dumpster! Anyway, I spent all afternoon exploring this amazing garden before continuing the road trip to Boston to visit my high school friend Elizabeth for a few days.

Elizabeth and I brought her baby Caroline to Boston Common where we met with Cheryl and her deaf baby Stephanie. With a smile, I figured that those two new mothers would have plenty to talk about. Caroline and Stephanie were only four months apart and there I found something absorbing about these two babies, one hearing and one deaf. I watched how they acted, showing a vast difference in their behaviors. Because she could hear all the environmental sounds, Caroline was much more vigorous than Stephanie, who just stared ahead in a pensive way. With chirping birds and yakking pedestrians around her, Caroline continued thrashing around in her stroller as if she wondered what all these sounds were, unlike Stephanie who didn't even know they existed. I added this interesting observation to all the others I had collected on this trip.

After saying good-bye to Elizabeth, I followed Cheryl to her apartment where she showed me all the special devices that would alert her to Stephanie's crying or whatever the baby was doing. Cheryl pointed to a monitor on the wall behind Stephanie's crib and intentionally made a sound. Sure enough, the hall light flicked on and so did the one in the master bedroom. Cheryl informed me that these lights would also turn on to the sounds of the phone ringing, the doorbell buzzing, and the smoke detector squealing. This deaf family certainly wouldn't miss anything important or dangerous.

Cheryl announced that Diane would call that evening to make plans for the reunion and that I would use a TTY for the first time. I'd seen a picture of this device in a magazine so I wasn't surprised by its resemblance to a typewriter. Cheryl explained that the red signal light would flash slowly, indicating the ringing of the other line. The typed conversation would appear in green-lighted words across the screen. Typing could cause the conversation to drag, so Cheryl told me I should use abbreviations or just single letters such as *u* for *you* and *q* for a question mark or for the word *question*. She explained two commonly used abbreviations that would help the other person know whether I had finished talking or was prepared to hang up: "GA" for "Go ahead" and "SK" for "Stop keying."

As promised, Diane phoned, and I was so frazzled with excitement that Cheryl had to keep reminding me how to use the TTY. I just couldn't believe I was actually "talking" to a deaf friend as I typed with shaking hands. I remember one part of our conversation perfectly. It went like this:

"WHERE CAN I MEET U ON FRIDAYQ THE SCHEDULE SAYS THERE WILL BE AN AFTERNOON RECEPTION. GA," I asked Diane regarding the reunion.

"I'LL JUST MEET U THERE. SHOULD BE AROUND 4 OR 5. DONT WAIT FOR ME CUZ THERE WILL BE OLD FRIENDS YOU HAVENT SEEN IN AGES. GA," Diane typed back rapidly, causing the words to zoom across the screen.

"OKIEDOKIE. TTY IS GREAT!!!!! WILL HAVE TO BUY ONE. SEE U AT THE RECEPTION. BYE BYE SK." I stopped with a grin while Cheryl patted me on the shoulder.

"BYE BYE OXOXO SKSK." The TTY's red, unblinking light then signaled that Diane had hung up. I made a promise to buy one for myself, ecstatic about the possibility of contacting Cheryl and Diane more frequently, rather than by mail.

Before my departure, Cheryl and I made plans on where to meet at the reunion. Just then, she told me not to get too excited about seeing our old friends because a majority of them were now signing. I felt my heart slump at her direct-eye warning that they could be hostile to me for maintaining oralism. Cheryl went on to tell me not to let them hurt my feelings and just to have a good time. Belonging now to the Deaf community (*Deaf* with a capital *D* to represent deaf culture and language), she could've acted the same way these friends would, but our friendship was too special to dissolve on account of different worlds.

But still, I was totally perplexed while driving to Northampton. All those friends were now signing? Why would they give up oralism if they had attended Clarke for years? Were they really in the Deaf community? I tried to imagine the possible difference between our past and present times. I cringed at the thought of my old friends looking at me in disgrace and asking, "Why are you still oral?" I had known that some people in the Deaf community could be quite harsh on those who chose to speak. They could be so fanatical about sign language that moving lips repulsed or even infuriated them—a total reverse of how the majority world had perceived sign language before 1960s, treating it then as taboo.

Thinking about all this, I became deeply concerned about seeing my old friends at the reunion. I'd be hurt like hell if they avoided me once they learned I had remained an oralist. After moments of pondering, I vowed to tell my friends immediately why I hadn't learned to sign. I'd just tell the truth: I was from Virginia where there weren't many deaf people for me to meet, not as many as in Massachusetts. And I had my hearing family help me through regular school, so I ended up fully immersed in the hearing world.

I also tried to understand why people, after learning oral methods for years, suddenly switched to sign. My mind turned to Cheryl who claimed that she had long felt miserably isolated in the hearing world and that she didn't learn much until her first year at NTID. She was, and is, profoundly deaf with approximately 88 percent hearing loss, compared to my 75 percent loss. There is an enormous difference between these two figures, even with powerful amplification. Cheryl cannot hear a teacup shattering on the floor like I can. She cannot talk on the phone with hearing friends like I can. No wonder Cheryl had to constantly struggle in the hearing world, only to find herself even more isolated. I just didn't understand all this when I first learned she had joined the Deaf community. Now I had grown to respect her choice of lifestyle if that was the reason she no longer felt lonely.

So maybe that's why many of my old friends had made the same choice—because they were profoundly deaf, not hard of hearing like me and Diane. But some profoundly deaf people actually belong to the hearing world with great success. Mark my word, every single deaf person is different, regardless of his or her degree of hearing loss. Some hard of hearing people even belong to the Deaf community, but only after they become fluent in American Sign Language.

On the first night of the reunion, we had a kickoff party where I reunited with some of my old classmates. Later, I joined them at a downtown bar and couldn't help feeling isolated when everyone was signing, although they could still lipread. One guy turned to me with a sheepish shrug and said that he wished I could sign. I must have looked chagrined when he told me not to be upset and reminded me of our capability to lipread. His words reassured me but I couldn't handle staying much longer and announced that I was heading back to the hotel.

Feeling letdown, I sat at the edge of the bed and wondered if I would have a good time with nearly everyone signing. I had realized that these old friends didn't really lipread those who signed to them, even though they still mouthed words. So maybe I could still communicate with them by using a combination of lipreading and hand gestures, even if my gestures weren't official sign language. It was better than nothing. I was not going to let myself sulk throughout the reunion.

Fortunately, the next day was better because more people who still lipread showed up, and I had long intense conversations with some of them. My explanation for not knowing sign language must have worked because many of my old friends were still super friendly and even taught me a few signs. Diane showed up later, afterward staying at the hotel with me, and Cheryl came for the day. Their presence made the reunion much more pleasant for me.

I found that, after graduating from Clarke, many of my friends were miserable or unsuccessful in the hearing world and therefore rejoined their deaf counterparts for a sense of belonging, somehow blending in with those who never went to Clarke, possibly at NTID or Gallaudet. After recognizing sign language as a definite remedy for miscommunication, these friends angrily felt that they had wasted time on oralism. That's the big reason several of them expressed resentment toward Clarke, calling it "too strict" or "unfair." These were the words I repeatedly heard during the reunion. A few of these friends even declared they would never forgive their hearing parents for sending them to the wrong school.

Honestly, if I were in their shoes, I would not be angry with my parents. Mom and Dad were the parents of the '60s, a time when sign language was considered repulsive. I would forgive my parents if they unintentionally deprived me of the most suitable communication method, not knowing how difficult the future would become. Cheryl, now in the Deaf community, had always been a realistic person and therefore knew that her parents were only trying to do the best for her.

When I came home and told people about how many of my friends had turned against Clarke, detesting its strict oral program, they each asked me the same question: Why did those people go to the reunion? My response was that they came because of *friends*. At the reunion, I watched how everyone expressed strong affection toward each other, giving bear hugs. The bonds, despite all the communication issues, were still strong.

I have to remind myself that every deaf person is different, no matter what the degree of hearing loss is. The truth is, not all deaf children can learn to speak well. That's what happened with many of my profoundly deaf friends. So I don't blame them for being angry that the early part of their lives had been wasted on oralism because that's the phase when language development is most significant. I can see why these friends feel they had missed a great deal of language through time-consuming oralism.

In spite of all this, I strongly support Clarke as an oral school. Although it could be extremely strict in the past, it was just doing its job teaching children to speak. I can understand why it didn't want the interference of sign language if its goal was to prepare students for the hearing world. Oralism was big during the 1960s and 1970s, but now it has changed. At the time of the reunion, Clarke's enrollment had been cut in half. But this school is still very much alive today because it now offers a wide variety of educational sessions throughout the country.

While driving home, I thought about all the events I had encountered over the last two weeks on this incredible trip. I was pleased with how the Clarke reunion had turned out, although I sorely wished that I had known sign language. The deaf world out there was totally different, something I did not expect at all. I felt a pang of desire to learn more about my own disability. Could there be so much about deafness that I still didn't know? It was definitely a mysterious disability, one of the most misunderstood disabilities to everyone, even myself.

Finally, I made two plans before arriving home, the first of which was to learn more about deafness by reading books, maybe meet local people associated with deafness and get their modern ideas, which had to be more flexible than those during the 1960s.

And the second plan— to learn sign language seriously so I would be able to communicate with deaf people—would not affect my oral skills one single bit. I could not wait to put these plans into action, pushing my foot a little further down on the pedal.

AT EASE

I had purchased a TTY and was now able to communicate with Cheryl and Diane through the phone lines. I also had purchased an American Sign Language book, trying to follow each picture of a signer with my awkward hands. I began to realize the liveliness and beauty of sign language, which motivated me to ask my audiologist Angela Sheppard about sign language classes. Angela, who has been a great lunch friend of mine all these years, has had to repair my broken tubes or listen to my complaints that manufacturers should invent sweat-proof hearing aids. (Oh, how nice those would be for playing competitive tennis!)

When I first met Angela, I was taken aback by her young age and even thought she was an earmold maker. My retiring audiologist had referred me to Angela's firm, saying "Ms. Sheppard" would help me. I had set up an appointment, assuming that my new audiologist would be about forty-five, slightly grey haired, and maybe pleasantly plump. That was what all the Clarke teachers had looked like, I remembered with fondness.

When I arrived at Ms. Sheppard's office, an attractive blond girl in her mid-twenties greeted me with a smile and asked what she could do for my hearing aid. After I hesitantly explained that the tube needed a replacement, she took my aid and disappeared. I sat there wondering where Ms. Sheppard was. Then the girl returned with a new tube and I asked very politely about my new audiologist. She looked at me in surprise and said she was the one. Caught off guard, I stared at her, thinking, That's *her*? Nah! I mean, this person was a *girl*, not the forty-five-year-old lady I expected. I realized that, despite my stereotyped expectations, anybody could be associated with deafness.

Anyway, Angela gave me a brochure of TAHIC (Tidewater Association for Hearing Impaired Children), a local deaf organization, so I could get information on sign language classes. I decided to join TAHIC just to meet interesting people, hearing or deaf. Since the Clarke reunion, I had a strong desire to learn more about deafness and believed that any TAHIC event would help broaden my knowledge of viewpoints.

I attended a Christmas party for deaf children and spoke with many hearing parents, most of whom could sign fluently. A majority of those children had cochlear implants and I couldn't keep my eyes off the steering-wheel magnet behind their ears. It was the first time I had seen a cochlear implant up close. Years before, Mom and I went to my ear doctor to discuss the possibility of a cochlear implant. It was so new at the time that we wondered if it was going to be a miracle for me. After giving me a hearing test, the doctor concluded that I wouldn't need an implant if I had enough help from my hearing aid. He explained that cochlear implants were particularly designed for those who could not be helped by amplification.

It turned out that most of the children at that party were in mainstream programs, attending regular schools that provided sign language interpreters and special classes. Regardless of their education methods, some of them could speak while others chose not to. I was elated with the atmosphere of mixed communication: sign language, oralism, and Cued Speech. The scene was a clear picture of diversity where everyone seemed happy with the chosen method of communication. There were people of all races: White, Black, Asian, Hispanic, and so on. I was psyched to learn sign and maybe Cued Speech, not just to develop the ability to communicate but also to broaden my perception of a disability with numerous controversial and sensitive issues.

While taking a sign language class, I learned that the two common signed languages in the United States were American Sign Language (ASL) and Signed Exact English (SEE). ASL, the number one signed language in the Deaf community, is actually a cultural language rich with beauty and fascination. It differs from SEE by having its own grammar and syntax. ASL uses signs, facial expressions, and body position to communicate concepts, defining objects, actions, and ideas with hand pictures and gestures. Sometimes, one ASL sign can express an entire sentence. ASL is a lot like French; in this sign language, an action or object comes first and a person comes last: Today store go me or Party give she. SEE, on the other hand, takes the English language, every bit of it, including all the little verb endings like *ing* and *ed*, and literally translates it into manual gestures.

Deaf people prefer ASL over English because it is much quicker and flows smoothly. The sign order of ASL allows them to rapidly form pictures or thoughts in their minds. It is difficult to be patient with the exact word order of Signed English where every small word must be included. I've heard negative comments from some deaf people and even interpreters, calling this method "slow" and "boring." Undoubtedly, deaf people feel more motivated with ASL, enjoying its speedy pace for social conversations.

But ASL is not without controversy. Opponents claim that this language prevents normal development in reading and writing skills and that ASL does not help with education. No book or closed captions are written in ASL. And very few hearing people actually use ASL. Therefore, opponents believe ASL causes deeper isolation of deaf people in the larger world.

Because of its quick and colorful way to communicate, I strongly support ASL, but I also believe that the English language should be a part of deaf culture. Understanding the English language's word order would enhance the ability to read warnings, instructions, and closed captions as well as books and magazines.

Personally, I would hate for deaf people to miss things they could easily learn with their perfectly normal minds.

Fortunately, there is a solution; it is a bilingual and bicultural system in which ASL is considered the first language and English the second. I strongly support this education method for deaf children if they are going to be raised in ASL. It is difficult to teach deaf toddlers the English language. However, with ASL, you can teach them their first words and help them identify pictures and people—all in a heartbeat. Then, these children can learn English through ASL. When they write, they can translate from ASL to English. When they read, they can translate from English to ASL. Most people can learn two different languages and cultures at the same time, for example, immigrants who speak English at school yet maintain their native tongues at home. The same is true with the bilingual-bicultural education involving ASL and English. Most important of all, this system helps build a bridge between deaf and hearing people.

I'm still not fluent in American Sign Language because its syntax is complicated. However, I use a combination of ASL and SEE; that's called Pidgin Sign English (PSE) in which you basically follow English word order but make shortcuts by eliminating small words such as *the* or *to*. And, like in ASL, I usually show physical language; for example, for the question mark, I raise my eyebrows or shrug my shoulders in a curious fashion. In fact, facial and body expressions are an absolute must for deaf people, whether speaking or signing, because they can't vary tones when using their voices to express feelings. Americans are more reserved with these physical aspects of language than Europeans; that's why Americans usually recoil or stare at deaf people who sign with one another using a variety of facial expressions. Deaf people just *have* to be that way, always making faces. Archie Bunker or Lucille Ball would have understood.

Now heavily involved in TAHIC, I realized that 90 percent of deaf children come from hearing families. And unfortunately, not all of these parents have the patience or "the time" to learn sign language or even to talk slowly to their deaf children; they just send them off to be mainstreamed at elementary schools, expecting the teachers to take care of everything. Sometimes, they send them to the closest deaf school, expecting the same of teachers there. It's true that deaf children often feel isolated in their families, unable to communicate with their parents and siblings who don't even try to understand anything about deafness.

Considering the 90 percent of deaf children coming from hearing families, only a handful of their parents are attentive enough to improve the mainstreaming education by meeting with school officials. I got to know these TAHIC parents personally, admiring them for their caring, even though raising a deaf child is not so easy.

In spite of all their immersion in deafness, it is unlikely that the hearing parents know what it is like being deaf. At one meeting, I spoke with a young mother whose deaf son kept interrupting our conversation. After he ran off, the mother apologized for his behavior. I brushed it off with understanding and asked if she had figured out why deaf children usually interrupt conversation. To my surprise, she had not. Of course, I had to explain that, because deaf children don't hear low conversation, they figure no one is talking. It's just a simple thing anyone can figure out about deafness.

One time, I was the only deaf person serving on the TAHIC board and had trouble understanding, despite the interpreter. I was so confused when the other members threw an assignment on my lap, giving the name of speaker to contact by phone. I didn't even know who that person was or what I was supposed to say to him. So I stormed out of the meeting, throwing up my arms. One of the members came out to ask what was wrong. I expressed my anger and frustration for not understanding what was going on. She nodded and admitted that she and the board members were not always deaf-friendly, especially during intense discussions. With a weary smile from the corner of my mouth, I told her they all *had* to be because of their deaf children. My point is, even excellent hearing professionals and parents of deaf children make thoughtless communication mistakes because they are not deaf.

If it weren't for TAHIC, I wouldn't have been able to collect all the astounding details about deafness. In truth, I had known very little about my own disability. I began to read numerous books on deafness, some medical and others biographical. Much to my surprise, I finally learned why my voice had always sounded foreign, even though I knew my vocal cords were normal. And I learned why my language development had taken so long to catch up. The more I learned, the more I appreciated my own life as a deaf person. I was finally at ease with my disability.

TAHIC had an annual weekend camp in which people came for workshops and the kids came for fun. Parents, educators, and interpreters took courses on topics such as child psychology and the individual education plan (or IEP). As a volunteer for children's activities, I took these kids canoeing and rope climbing. Because most families who attended brought all their members, there were hearing siblings interacting with deaf children in all age groups. It was a wonderful connection because all these kids could communicate in sign language.

One time, I attended a Cued Speech camp, just to learn this unusual type of communication. Cued Speech is a simple, sound-based system, using eight hand shapes in four different positions that combine with the motions of the lips to make visible and clearly understandable all the sounds of the English language. So the reader of Cued Speech would be able to distinguish "man," "bat," and "pad," even if he or she were completely deaf. In fact, this method, along with lipreading, enables a deaf person to see exactly what a hearing person hears.

At camps, I learned a great deal about the Deaf community, which is really diverse. Not everyone has the same views and outlooks. There are indeed different groups of deaf people. Some speak; others don't. Some read well; others don't. Some support Total Communication; others don't. Some are understanding of hearing people; others are not. But still, the Deaf community is like a big family absorbed in one language, American Sign Language.

From what I had witnessed at camps, the Deaf community is a close-knit group full of love and friendship. Unlike the hearing culture, these deaf people form strong bonds, expressing affection with hugs and long good-byes. Because they live in the midst of a larger world with all kinds of people, Deaf people tend to linger on at a social gathering, hesitant to leave where they feel they most belong. In fact, the Deaf culture is so unusual and unpretentious that the larger world doesn't even know it exists.

People are often puzzled with the fierceness of the Deaf community. That fierceness has developed because the community desperately wants to save its diminishing culture and is especially upset with the cochlear implant, perceiving it as a clash with its culture. As a matter of fact, the Deaf community wants to prove that many people are perfectly happy without hearing aids. These people declare that the cochlear implant won't work for everyone. They aren't the only ones with this viewpoint, however. Even some doctors and professionals admit that the implant is not for every deaf person; hearing losses can vary in so many complex ways. The implant does work for some people, especially the older ones who want their hearing back, although the sounds coming from it are indeed different from the normal ear. And some prelingually deaf children grow up successfully with the cochlear implant, happy to hear only environmental sounds, while others just throw it away, declaring that they do not need to hear. That's why the cochlear implant poses a huge dilemma for most hearing parents of deaf newborns.

Meeting several of the signing people at meetings and camps, I learned that the Deaf community supports its own members better than the hearing world supports those who are deaf within it. Deaf children raised by deaf parents don't feel inferior when facing the harsh reality of the everyday world. In addition, these children, often attending deaf schools, are able to learn warnings early through signed language, so they're likely to be less naive than the deaf children relying on the hearing world. (Tell me about it!) That's because deaf families can communicate with each other more completely.

However, that richer communication happens not only in deaf families but also in families with deaf parents and hearing children. Two interesting people I met at one of the camps were Yvonne and April: a deaf mother and her hearing daughter. Yvonne, immersed in the Deaf community heart and soul, told me how she taught her daughter to stand up to neighborhood bullies. She signed "Stand up [for] yourself!" by standing two fingertips in a V—two legs standing proudly—on her upturned palm (Stand up!) and then, with her thumb rising from a fist, thrusting her hand toward April with great force (Yourself). Obviously, it had worked because April was as tough as her mother was, though they didn't belong in the same worlds.

While April volunteered with me at the camp, she told me about her past experiences fiercely protecting her deaf mother, even as a little girl. She proudly regaled her stories of getting into physical fights with kids who ridiculed her deaf mother. Awestruck by her courage, I asked April if she ever felt embarrassed about having a deaf mother. She replied no because Yvonne's strong character taught her that deaf people were real human beings and didn't deserve such ignorance and mockery.

Some hearing people don't realize deaf people can feel and think like them. They often think deaf people are merely hollow statues. No, no, no. Deaf people's feelings and thoughts run deep. If they are supported and encouraged early, deaf children can grow up to be confident and curious, testing things around them and exploring what others think.

My husband Steve once underwent outpatient knee surgery and waited at the door with a hospital nurse while I went to pick up our car. When I pulled up, the nurse frowned at Steve and asked, "Your wife can drive?" Well, of course! And I remember playing badminton years ago and someone approached, looking me up and down skeptically and asking how I could play. I mean, really. All you have to do is whack that little birdie over the net. Well, I have a message for those who think deaf people don't know how to do things. Let me put it this way: I'll be polite, but I want to let you know that we deaf people are not stupid. We know how to drink tequila the right way, using lemon and salt. We know how to smoke a fat cigar and roll the dice across the poker table— and even win the pot. We know how to sneak into a neighbor's pool at midnight for a marvelous nude swim. We know how to neck all night on the beach before going much further. We can be as resourceful and clever as anybody. Please note that deaf people are normal-minded human beings. Thank you.

I was amazed to learn how controversial this disability really is, possibly the most controversial of all. I cannot think of any other disability that is as intense: Oralism versus Sign Language, American Sign Language versus Signed Exact English, Cochlear Implant versus Deaf Culture, Mainstreaming versus Special Education. Learning more about deafness had made me less ashamed of what I'd experienced since birth. The wall around me had now crumbled down and I was willing to reveal all the deep feelings about being deaf in a hearing world, especially in the past.

Not too long after a terrible breakup with another guy, I went to dinner at a restaurant with a small group of friends and met the man who would become my husband. As we mingled within this small group, it became clear that we were obviously attracted to each other. After chatting with him for a few hours, I assumed that Steve knew about my deafness. But he didn't; he later asked one of our friends why I kept looking at his teeth. The friend gaped at Steve and exclaimed, "She is deaf! She was reading your lips!" On our second date, Steve shared that, on that first night, he had been so worried that he had some green vegetable stuck between his teeth.

With my husband Steve and our two dogs
Olive, left, and Mabel in 2001.

Now we have been married sixteen years, and we often marvel at our successful hearing-deaf relationship. I believe that our four years of dating helped foster patience and understanding on Steve's part. Since I knew most hearing-deaf marriages did not work, I asked Steve four or five times with a cautious look on my face if he was absolutely positive that he would tolerate living with a deaf person. Each time, Steve explained that he knew all along that he would be the one who needed to adjust to my disability; that's why I felt confident about marrying him. When we first started dating, we took the necessary time and had the needed patience to develop a trusting relationship, especially one involving a hearing impaired person. Most important, Steve and I knew that love and respect would grow, not just pop out of the blue. That love and respect did grow for us, and it was worth the wait and the patience.

Soon after Steve and I settled in at his house, newly married, he became perplexed about how I detected sounds around the house. Shortly after our honeymoon, I was boiling eggs and eventually forgot about them while cleaning the house. Before long, the smoke detector seemed to emit a high-pitched sound, which I heard off and on. What I mean by "off and on" is a tricky characteristic of nerve deafness. I couldn't tell whether the high-pitched alarm was an actual sound or just an echoing in my head. Fortunately, there was no fire, and I threw the scorched pot, along with the scalded eggs, out the door.

But then, I was uncertain about the sound of a smoke detector, so I grabbed a chair and stood on it and fiddled with the device, trying to turn off the red light. Being terribly naive about alarm systems, I wasn't sure if that light was supposed to stay on. Increasingly unsettled, I phoned Steve at work and told him to listen carefully. He did not reply. As he was listening, the red light on the smoke detector finally went off, perhaps because of my excess fiddling, and I said never mind, hanging up. Later in the evening, Steve came home, still puzzled, asking for my explanation. He then told me that he had heard no sound on the phone. These days he likes telling the story about how I stood up on a chair, holding the phone up to the soundless smoke detector.

It didn't take Steve long to understand that I can neither hear high-pitched sounds very well nor pinpoint where sounds come from. Every time he calls me from the other room, I hear him, but head the wrong way. At times, we go around and around inside the house until poor Steve stops his pursuit and wails, "I'm right here!" Sometimes, I stop in frustration and holler that he has to come over to me. We both know that, because of my little twisted auditory nerve, there is no way we can talk or holler to each other from different rooms as most married couples do. Back in college, my roommate was tapping her wet hairbrush on the edge of our little sink and I turned to the door in a light inviting tone, "Come in." That's nerve deafness for you!

One night, Steve and I took our yellow lab Olive for a walk, and our dog disappeared into the bushes yards away. After waiting, I wondered aloud if Olive had already done her business. Steve insisted that was what she was doing right at this moment. I stared at him doubtfully and asked, "Well, then how do you know if you can't see Olive taking a poop fifty feet away in the total dark?" With a huge grin, he explained that once our dog's tags stopped jiggling and the leaves stopped rustling, it was happening right there. I tell you, hearing people's hearing never ceases to amaze me.

Always a caring person, Steve has showed me how to ignore hurtful remarks and stand up to insensitive people. Once, we were in Boston, meeting with Cheryl and her family for a deaf walkathon along the Charles River. Hundreds of deaf people took over the whole pathway, but cyclists, runners, and rollerbladers were also flying by. One big guy yelled for everyone to scoot out of his way, "Hey, (bleep)! Get the (bleep) out of my way! Move! (Bleep)! Are they deaf or what? (Bleep)!" My dear husband shot back, "Yes, you dumb (bleep)! They are deaf, (bleep)! This is a deaf walkathon! Why don't *you* move the (bleep) of the way!" Sure enough, the rollerblader slowed down with a surprised look and then tucked his head and rolled away.

Being married to Steve has given me a true identity in the hearing world. Before meeting him, I wasn't sure about belonging to the hearing culture 100 percent because I was rarely asked out by hearing guys and had such a difficult time finding a tolerant mate. Because I had spent years fighting so hard for acceptance and finally found happiness with work and social life in the hearing world, I didn't want to throw it all away by marrying a deaf guy. In truth, I was fully set to marry a hearing guy and would wait forever if I had to. Maybe it was my relationship with my three brothers that prompted me to choose this kind of union; I was so familiar with hearing males. But I often worried that the man I would fall in love with would not get used to me as a deaf person. It was a disturbing feeling.

It is important for a deaf person to have a true identity, either in the Deaf community or in the hearing world. Unfortunately, many deaf and hard of hearing people feel torn between those opposite cultures, uncertain where they really belong. That conflict leads to zero self-esteem and severe depression, causing one to feel like a nobody. It is the worst feeling ever. The Deaf community does not accept those who don't know ASL fluently. And the hearing world does not readily accept all deaf and hard of hearing people. Therefore, many of these people are left in the middle without a sense of belonging. That's what happened to me when I was twenty-one. My sense of belonging was an off-and-on situation that gave me a roller-coaster emotional ride. One day was bad enough; a lifetime would be too hard to bear.

Hard of hearing people are likely to take the most abuse from both the Deaf community and the hearing world. The former shuns them, believing that they are not really "Deaf." And the hearing world either ignores them or expects too much of them while it tends to be more sympathetic with those who are profoundly deaf. You see, most hard of hearing people can speak and hear with amplification, so they are expected to be like hearing people. I've been through that before. The truth is, I can sometimes hear fully and clearly what is said behind my back, and other times, I can't. It just depends on the sound feedback or just my concentration. So really, people need to be gentler on hard of hearing people, most of whom are miserably struggling for a true identity, torn between the hearing world and the Deaf community. Actually it's even more difficult and more depressing to be hard of hearing than totally deaf.

While doing research, I was shocked to read that only 3 percent of hearing-deaf marriages actually work. But other books said 5 percent, 10 percent, and other small figures, so the exact percentage may never be known. (I'd be shocked if 25 percent of hearing-deaf marriages did work!) Anyway, I showed the book to Steve, pointing to the 3 percent in astonishment. He didn't react much, but the next day he came home with a dozen red roses and announced that he was delighted and proud "to be in the 3 percent." You can imagine tears in my eyes.

Because deafness is emotional and intense, I decided to give up a landscape design career for counseling. After designing landscapes for twenty years and trying unsuccessfully to have children, I felt something beckoning me: a chance to counsel people with a disability similar to mine. I dreamed of encouraging deaf clients to make the best of their disability and to lead productive, healthy lives. And also help reduce friction between deaf children and their hearing families—and yes, even between deaf and hearing spouses. I told myself that I would never give deaf clients advice on which type of communication or lifestyle to choose since it was entirely up to an individual. So then I achieved a master's degree in counseling at Old Dominion University in December 2004.

But then I ended up working with various disabilities, not just one. Therefore, I did not become a deaf counselor as expected; instead, I was offered a job coaching position in February 2006 by Hired Hands & Associates, an employment agency that assists people with disabilities in competitive employment. Anna Burns and her husband Tim started this agency in NYC after working at the Marriott hotel where there were deaf employees. Marriott had hired ten deaf individuals when the hotel opened in Times Square in 1985; that's when Anna, with her ASL interpreting skills, was hired in order to communicate with them. Tim was working at the same hotel as a human resources manager. During the Burns' four years there, the Marriott brought in fifty additional deaf people. That huge success prompted Anna and Tim to form Hired Hands to do placement and training in other NYC hotels. As luck would have it for me, they decided to move to Virginia in 1992 and continued employment services, now broadening their focus on other disabilities such as mental and physical challenges.

In fact, this is the best job I've ever had. It has made me more understanding and appreciative of a wide variety of disabilities such as Down's Syndrome and cerebral palsy. Job coaching is actually like counseling because many people with disabilities tend to allow their personal issues affect their work performance. I do try to keep these consumers employed as long as possible especially during this economical crisis. And also keep the lines of communication open between myself, the consumer, and his/her employer. No wonder I've often used sign language with deaf consumers, some of whom I have placed at retail stores, restaurants, and a military base throughout the area.

My main goal in writing this memoir is to build a bridge between hearing and deaf people. It is badly needed. Those two different groups can help one another understand their worlds. The Deaf community needs to be recognized for its own culture and language; therefore, it should not be eliminated altogether. The hearing culture needs to understand that deaf people are unlike them only in terms of their ears. Hearing and deaf people need to share. Hearing people shouldn't ignore deaf people, and deaf people shouldn't resent hearing people. Finally, this memoir has another goal: to encourage the majority to learn and appreciate a disability of any kind in general.

It's time to break ground and get to work. We need to build a bridge and cross it soon. It has been too long.